WILLIAM
THE PEOPLE'S PRINCE

WILLIAM
THE PEOPLE'S PRINCE

IAN LLOYD

PAVILION

DEDICATION
FOR SHARON MURRAY,
WHO MADE THIS POSSIBLE

First published in Great Britain in 2003 by
Pavilion Books Limited

A member of **Chrysalis** Books plc

The Chrysalis Building
Bramley Road
London, W10 6SP

Text © Ian Lloyd 2003
Design and layout © Pavilion Books 2003
The moral right of the author has been asserted

Designed by Nigel Partridge

A CIP catalogue record for this book is available from the
British Library.

ISBN 1 86205 572 6

Set in Granjon, Trajan and Helvetica

Colour reproduction by Classicscan Pte Limited, Singapore
Printed and bound in Portugal by Printer Portuguesa

1 3 5 7 9 10 8 6 4 2

This book may be ordered direct from the publisher.
Please contact the marketing department.
But try your bookshop first.

CONTENTS

A FAMILY TREE SHOWING THE DESCENT OF PRINCE WILLIAM FROM THE HOUSE OF WINDSOR AND FROM THE SPENCER FAMILY

Through his mother Diana, Princess of Wales, Prince William is descended five times from the illegitimate children of Charles II and his brother James II, bringing the romantic blood of the Stuarts back into the royal line. Recent generations of Diana's family maintained close links with the royal family. Her two grandmothers, Lady Cynthia Spencer and Ruth, Lady Fermoy, both held the position of Woman of the Bedchamber to Queen Elizabeth the Queen Mother. Her grandfather Lord Fermoy was a close friend of William's great grandfather King George VI, and Diana's father, Earl Spencer, was an equerry to the present Queen at the time of her accession. Finally, William's uncle Sir Robert Fellowes was the Queen's private secretary from 1990 to 1999, a position that led to divided family loyalties following the separation of the Prince and Princess of Wales.

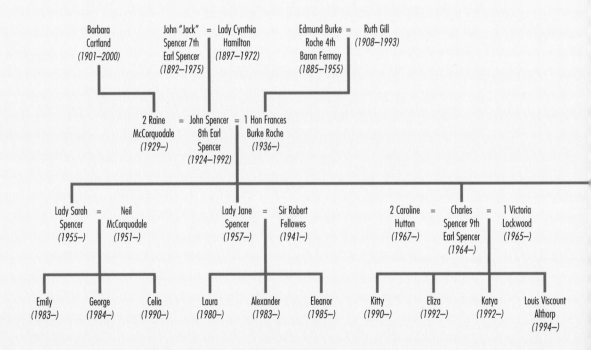

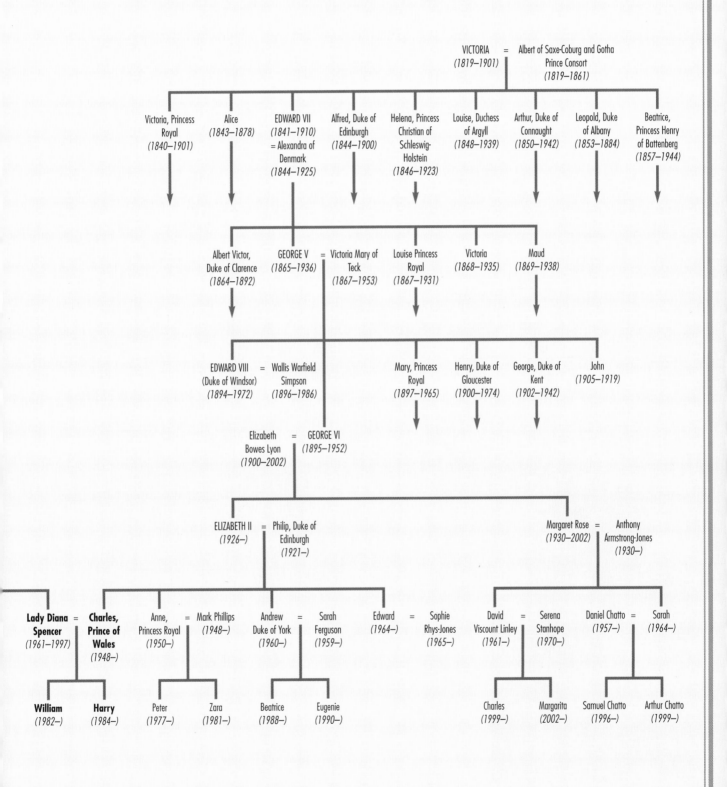

INTRODUCTION

The moment William Arthur Philip Louis came kicking and screaming into the centre of an affluent west London family on a balmy June evening in 1982 his fate was already decided. The blissfully unaware blue-eyed, blond-haired baby would, in all probability, succeed his father as the twenty-second Prince of Wales. Further along the royal road – barring death, revolution or devolution – he would eventually become His Majesty King William V, the forty-second monarch since the Norman Conquest.

One day thirty, forty or fifty years hence William will be meeting and greeting kings, ambassadors, bishops, generals and MPs. He will, among other things, offer advice to successive Prime Ministers, review troops, open parliament, broadcast to the nation and personally award two thousand MBEs, OBEs and CBEs annually.

He will tour Britain time and again, he will welcome heads of state and will later return their visits in a diplomatic tit for tat. In all situations he will endeavour to be polite, friendly, sincere, apolitical and uncontroversial.

His destiny is a world of immense wealth and privilege. Besides castles and palaces he will one day presumably inherit the vast estates of Sandringham and Balmoral as well as his father's Highgrove mansion. He will own one of the finest private art collections as well as the world famous stamp collection begun by King George V. He will have a fleet of official limousines at his disposal, and vaults full of jewels, gold plate and porcelain.

Right: William is the monarchy's golden hope for the future. The royal spin doctors and image makers can breathe a sigh of relief that here is a prince who has caught the public imagination single-handed.

Left: The royal superstar. The combination of his mother's stunning good looks, his father's athleticism, and his vulnerability following Diana's death have combined to create the ultimate pin-up prince.

While the critics will always focus on William's wealth and privilege, supporters will point out that a life of luxury is far from commensurate for taking on a role that was signed and sealed at birth. Whether he succeeds as king or forfeits his birthright for a life in exile, William will forever live in the spotlight. He will be dogged by the press, flattered by would-be friends and associates, betrayed by former contacts and tailed by a phalanx of security men.

He will never be able to forge a career that is suitable for his talents or interests. Any burning desire to be a professional footballer, polo player,

Above: A carefree day at Thorpe Park in April 1993. Diana tried to give her sons a glimpse of a normal life Although her life would be brutally ended four years later, her influence on the princes and the future of the monarchy is likely to remain for all time.

artist, violinist or whatever will never reach fruition. At best he will compromise between royal life and his other interests in a similar way to his aunt, the Princess Royal, who represented Britain in three-day eventing at the 1976 Montreal Olympics.

At twenty-one, William is already one of only a handful of VIPs whose Christian name alone is instantly recognizable the world over in newspaper headlines, on magazine covers and on websites. There will be a plethora of books, magazines, newspaper tributes and documentaries to mark his coming of age. All of them will celebrate the life of a young man whose few public appearances guarantee an adulation not seen since the days of Di-mania. At the same time, he remains the most private of men.

We know that he has led a fairly blameless life on the pre-school, prep school road that took him to Eton and on to St Andrews University. Despite being cloistered behind the redbrick shield of college walls and the even grander seclusion of palaces, William has still managed to capture the public's imagination and at twenty-one has already firmly established himself in several roles.

The aim of this book is to look at each of those roles in turn and to show how he has succeeded in them, emerging as a credit to his family and as an inspiration to his undeniably huge fan base.

We will see how William's personality has been shaped by his relationships with his immediate family. His mother Diana, Princess of Wales, taught him to communicate effectively with people of all classes and to learn how the age-old institution of monarchy can have a positive impact in helping the scourges of drug abuse, homelessness and AIDS-related illnesses, as well as the previously neglected plight of landmine victims. Through Diana he was also aware of the downside of royal life. He witnessed at first hand the intense scrutiny that she was always under from the media and her fans. He saw how frustrating it was to her free spirit to be constrained in a world of servants, police and protection officers. In her final years William was also to witness the difficulties she faced as a royal princess in virtual exile, no longer an HRH, dropped from official prayers and with no official role to play in state events. All of this would shape his future vision and attitude to monarchy.

Left: William's clear-cut profile suggests strength of mind and a determined personality. By the time he was pictured here at the age of nineteen he was developing a firmly controlled, independent streak that is likely eventually to charcterize his role as king.

From his father, William has developed a sensitive appreciation of art, literature, architecture and the environment, particularly farming.

Charles has seen how frustrating the role of king in waiting can be, with no clear constitutional role other than to support the Queen. Trying to carve a career as Prince of Wales at the beginning of the twenty-first century is an unenviable task. His Prince's Trust is an undoubted success and one that William may try to emulate. His outspoken espousal of other causes have met with mixed reactions from the media and from specialists in these areas. William has seen at first hand how this "jack of all trades, master of none" approach has its limitations and he may decide to involve himself in a few chosen causes such as the Prince's Trust or his mother's influential support for the abolition of landmines. This way he can have a real impact and avoid controversy.

His more spirited fun-loving brother Harry and his cousins Peter and Zara have, especially in the wake of Diana's death, provided a welcome safety-valve from the often rigid protocol of royal life, the intrusion of the media and the daunting scrutiny of the public.

Finally, there has been the influence of the older royal family – William's grandparents the Queen and Prince Philip – with their unshakeable belief in duty, protocol and public service. This was of course compounded by the influence of an even earlier generation, thanks to the legacy of the Queen Mother, who was born in the reign of Queen Victoria and who lived to see William reach his twentieth year. From her legendary image of wartime self-sacrifice William came to realize that royalty should lead by example rather than by theory. With her *joie de vivre* and exuberance she also taught him that royal life could and should also be fun.

We will see William in a variety of other roles. There's William the media star who, like his mother, can add twenty per cent to the circulation of most magazines simply by appearing on the cover. There's William the fashion icon, a reluctant pin-up prince from the age of thirteen. William the student – the most academically gifted of recent royals, and possibly the only royal prince to reach university on merit. Finally, there is William the sportsman, who has inherited his mother's love of swimming alongside the traditional House of Windsor hunting, shooting and fishing lifestyle.

Below: William, a man of his times. He has inherited both Charles and Diana's sensitive natures and can relate to all types of character. "I just hope I can meet people I get on with", he told one interviewer, "I don't care about their backgrounds".

In all of these areas we will look at how his parents, grandparents and other royal relations themselves made their own impact, and how they themselves celebrated this landmark birthday.

William at twenty-one is trying to lead as normal a life as possible. The royal round of duties and engagements is still far ahead of him, and for the moment he is living the life of a typical student. In his relatively short lifetime he has experienced the gamut from adulation to tragedy, and has won respect for the way he has coped with both extremes. This respect is a sound base from which to start his public life, no matter what challenges lie ahead.

CHAPTER ONE

WILLIAM
AND DIANA

She was the shy teenager who became an icon, the compassionate humanitarian ruled forever by her heart. She was adored by millions and could outshine the glitziest of Hollywood stars. She was married to the twenty-first Prince of Wales, but she was known the world over by one name – Diana. For just sixteen years she played a variety of parts from royal princess to media star, from fashion pin-up to charity worker. Yet without doubt her favourite role was that as a mother of two sons – "my boys" – one of whom will one day rule over the United Kingdom and whatever is left of its Commonwealth as King William V.

It all began so well in the baking heat of a late July morning. An estimated 750 million people worldwide watched as Lady Diana Spencer arrived at St Paul's Cathedral and began the three-and-a-half minute walk to her destiny. Leaning on the arm of her frail father, Earl Spencer, she walked down the 250-metre (625-foot) blue-carpeted aisle towards the man who had told us all that he was in love, "whatever love means". As the resounding strains of Jeremiah Clarke's "Trumpet Voluntary" died away, twenty-one sovereigns, twenty heads of state and twenty-six governors general watched intently as Diana exchanged a nervous smile with her future husband. Robert Runcie, the one-hundred-and-second archbishop of Canterbury, stepped forward to begin the service with the phrase that would reverberate down through the next two decades, "Here is the stuff of which fairy tales are made ...".

Diana, as a non-royal bride, was technically a commoner. In fact she

Right: Despite suffering from post-natal depression, Diana found natural fulfilment in motherhood. Here the princess poses with her son at Kensington Palace in the summer of 1982. William's first official photoshoot was conducted by the photographer Lord Snowdon, the former husband of Princess Margaret.

Left: Just thirty-six hours old, the prince makes his public debut outside London's St Mary's Hospital, Paddington. The proud parents had yet to settle on a name for the second in line to the throne, who was still known officially as "Baby Wales".

could trace her descent in four lines, albeit illegitimate ones, from Charles II (1630–85) and his mistresses and in one more from his brother James II (1633–1701). Add to that a distant kinship with Sir Winston Churchill and five US presidents – Calvin Coolidge, Franklin D. Roosevelt, both George Bushes and even George Washington – and it was more than apparent that Diana could pass on genes that would combine leadership with colourful Stuart romance.

By the early autumn of 1981 Diana knew she was pregnant, the first Princess of Wales to have a baby in nearly eighty years. Both parents were naturally euphoric. Charles stopped his honeymoon practice of reading her extracts from the Swiss psychologist Carl Jung and the philosopher Sir Laurens Van der Post, and began instead to pore over books on the even more daunting topics of childbirth and parenting. Charles and Diana turned up unexpectedly at a lecture on childbirth as well as attending breathing classes, which must have been a surreal distraction for all the other couples.

Pregnancy wasn't easy for the twenty-year-old princess, who later recalled in tapes sent to the writer Andrew Morton that she "couldn't sleep, didn't eat, whole world was collapsing around me. Very, very difficult pregnancy indeed ... almost every time I stood up I was sick." Even more distressing was the combined effect of morning sickness and the bulimia that was beginning to affect her.

William Arthur Philip Louis was born in St Mary's Hospital, Paddington, west London, as the sun was beginning to set at 9.03 p.m. on 21 June 1982, the longest day of the year. "Baby Wales", as he was known to the hospital staff, weighed 3.46 kg (7 lb 10 oz), had a wisp of blond hair and, most importantly of all for the royal dynasty, he was a son and heir. As if to emphasize this royal continuity, William was baptized on 4 August 1982, to honour Charles's adored grandmother, the Queen Mother, who was eighty-two that day. Few

Below: After William's birth, Charles declared himself "relieved, delighted, overwhelmed, over the moon". Diana was totally besotted with her son, describing herself as "thrilled and excited". Her friend Caroline Bartholomew noted a "contentment about her".

Above: A family photocall at Government House in New Zealand. Afterwards Charles wrote that the nine-month-old prince "is the greatest possible fun...he performed like a true professional in front of the cameras and did everything that could be expected of him".

present at the service in the music room of Buckingham Palace could have imagined that this elderly lady, born in 1900 while Queen Victoria was still alive, would go on to live to see William start his university career in his twentieth year.

Home for the new-born prince was an L-shaped, three-storey apartment in Kensington Palace. The Queen had given the Waleses two apartments (numbers 8 and 9), which they converted into one palatial unit with twenty-five principal rooms and many smaller ones. Diana spent the first year of her marriage renovating the interior, guided by South African designer Dudley Poplak. Together they designed a nursery for the top floor made up of three bedrooms, a playroom, a kitchen and a dining-room. This was to be William's main home for the next fifteen years.

Both Charles and Diana had troubled childhoods and Diana, in particular, was determined that William, and later his brother Harry, would receive constant, unconditional love from their parents. "Her affection for them was unmistakable", recalled her private secretary Patrick Jephson. "She was warm, expressive and tactile. Very obviously she wanted neither her boys nor anybody else to be in any doubt about her love for them." Diana found motherhood blissfully fulfiling, as she once revealed to Maudie Pendry, her father's former housekeeper. "William has brought us such happiness and contentment and consequently I can't wait to have masses more!"

With Diana and Charles in constant demand to carry out royal engagements, it was inevitable that they would both see less of William than they would like, and that most of his day would be spent with his nanny. The couple chose Barbara Barnes, the forty-two-year-old daughter of a forestry worker, who never wore a nursery uniform and liked the children to call her by her first name. William was only nine months old when, accompanied by Nanny Barnes, he joined his parents for their six-week tour of Australia and New Zealand, clocking up more than 30,000 miles of travel. In 1953 his grandmother, the Queen, had to make a similar tour by sea and was away from the five-year-old Charles for nearly nine months. Both Charles and Diana were determined that history shouldn't repeat itself, and the Queen backed their decision. While his parents toured Australia, William was based at Woomargama, a 4,000-acre sheep station in New South Wales. "We didn't see very much of him," recalled Diana later, "but at least we were under the same sky, so to speak."

Just a few weeks after their return from Australia and New Zealand to the United Kingdom, Charles and Diana went on tour again, this time to Canada. On this occasion they went without William, since it was considered too disruptive to take him abroad for just two weeks, particularly when his parents were not going to be based in one city. Because of the tour Diana was forced her to miss her son's first birthday – it cannot have been easy for the twenty-two-year-old, insecure mother to have to telephone Kensington Palace where her son was celebrating his birthday with a party across the Atlantic Ocean. Charles also had a word with his young son and, like Diana, was rewarded "with a few little squeaks". On a walkabout in Ottawa, Diana told the crowds, "I really am missing him. He is

a beautiful little boy, and we are both extremely proud of him."

He might have been a beautiful little boy when he was a year old, but by the time he was two he was running around Birkhall, the Queen Mother's Aberdeenshire home, creating havoc in the dining room and being cheeky to the servants. By the time he was four he was proving a handful. The list of his early antics is endless, from trying to flush his father's shoe down the lavatory to setting off the security alarms at nearby Balmoral Castle, the Queen's Scottish home, an act that sent police cars hurtling from Aberdeen to seal off the royal estate. On a visit to his Spencer relations at Althorp House in Northamptonshire he "frightened the life out of us", recalled Diana's father, "when he took a toboggan to the top of the grand staircase and whizzed all the way down."

"William is getting to be quite a handful," Diana revealed to another mother on a walkabout. She tried her best to discipline him, even smacking him on the bottom in public when she spotted him pushing a little girl to the ground at the Guards Polo Club in Windsor Great Park. Not surprisingly the tabloids were soon awarding him the distinctly unregal title of "Basher Billy".

Earl Spencer commented in an interview, "He's very high-spirited, tremendously energetic and always getting into trouble. But you can't get annoyed with him, however naughty he's been, because he's got such charm. For a five-year-old he's tremendously cunning, he knows how to get his own way." This would also have been an apt description for his great-aunt Princess Margaret, who Queen Mary described as *espiégle* "mischievous", but then admitted, "All the same she is so outrageously amusing that one can't help encouraging her." Margaret was to rebel for most of her life, but for the young prince it was just a juvenile phase, as his godmother Carolyn Bartholomew noticed. She said that at first she thought that William was a "little terror", but then commented, "Later, when I had my two children I realized they are all like that at some point."

Diana decided to take a firm hand with her son. When, at four-and-a-half, he started lessons at Wetherby School, a few minutes' drive from Kensington Palace, Diana appointed a new nanny to replace Barbara Barnes. Ruth Wallace, a former nanny to the children of ex-King Constantine of Greece, took up the role as head of the nursery with Olga Powell as her assistant. Nevertheless Diana still drove William, and later Harry, to and from school whenever possible, and back at Kensington Palace she would bath them and read to them.

When they went away to school, it was Olga who packed their suitcases and trunks as well as ensured that they had enough snacks in their tuck-boxes. Miss Powell said at the trial of Paul Burrell – Diana's butler – in October 2002 that Diana tried to look after the boys as much as possible, and wanted them to live as normal a life as possible. She encouraged them to mix with the children of her staff, including Burrell's two sons Alexander and Nicholas, and she organized barbecues for them at Highgrove, the estate in Gloucestershire that Charles had bought just before his marriage.

Charles and Diana were keen to ensure that William and Harry enjoyed the secure, emotionally stable family environment that neither of them had experienced. However, although the couple were co-operating with television documentaries, photoshoots and books that projected the positive image of a happy marriage, the reality was very different. "We were very, very close to each other the six weeks before Harry was born," Diana recalled in the early 1990s, "the closest we've ever, ever been and ever will be. Then,

Below: Walking confidently into the future. A walk in the countryside for William, Diana, Harry and other members of the Spencer family, including the princes' grandmother Mrs Frances Shand Kydd. A relaxed William had yet to enter his camera-shy teenage years.

Right: Applause for papa. William and Diana offer loyal support to Charles during a polo match at Smith's Lawn on the Queen's Windsor estate. These were among the happiest days of the royal marriage and Diana frequently took the boys to watch their father play.

suddenly, as Harry was born (in September 1984) it just went bang, our marriage, the whole thing went down the drain."

The Queen felt that the root of the problem was Charles's inability to cope with Diana's bulimia, the eating disorder that had plagued her through her courtship, wedding and pregnancies. Her father argued that Diana, a bride, a royal princess and a mother all before she was twenty-one, had simply not had the time to adjust to any of these roles. "There are times when I wish she could have a couple of years off to bring up her children, be at home with them and not worry about anything else apart from them and her husband," he commented when William was five, adding, "Instead it's a bit like a non-stop circus."

The marriage deteriorated steadily from 1986 to the end of the decade. During one six-week period the couple spent only one day together. The Buckingham Palace press office consistently denied rumours of a rift.

According to Patrick Jephson, Diana was concerned about the negative newspaper reports, admitting, "Never far from her thoughts was the potential effect on Princes William and Harry." Her concern was justified. "William was by now old enough to be aware of the rows and tensions in

Right: In August 1987 Charles, Diana and the boys join the Spanish royal family for a holiday at the Marivent Palace on Majorca. In exchange for a week's privacy the two families pose for photographs on the palace steps at the beginning of their break. Five-year-old William looks as though he'd rather be on the beach.

Left: Six-year-old William and four-year-old Harry pose with Diana for a photoshoot at Highgrove to mark Charles's fortieth birthday in 1988. The Prince of Wales is off-camera and pulling faces to make his family laugh.

his parents' marriage," observed Wendy Barry, the housekeeper at Highgrove. "No amount of play-acting can ever fool a child."

The marriage reached its crisis point in the summer of 1992 when, in the week of William's tenth birthday, Andrew Morton's book *Diana, Her True Story* was serialized in *The Sunday Times*. Written with the co-operation of Diana's friends (and, as became apparent after her death, Diana herself), the book gave a detailed account of Diana's struggle with bulimia, her suicide attempts and the re-emergence in Charles's life of Camilla Parker-Bowles. At Ludgrove Preparatory School, William and Harry were shielded from the controversy as much as possible. Staff were briefed to hide tabloid newspapers and to discourage other pupils from talking about what the rest of the country seemed to be obsessed with.

A final family holiday – a cruise off the Greek islands – only exacerbated the situation. Charles, Diana and the boys were joined by the Queen's cousin Princess Alexandra, her husband Sir Angus Ogilvy and other friends on board the *Alexander*, a yacht owned by the Greek billionaire John Latsis.

According to Andrew Morton, "Diana kept herself to herself, having little contact with her husband, sleeping in a separate cabin and preferring to take her meals with the children." The tension must have been awful for William and Harry and, according to their detective Ken Wharfe, who was with them, "They became concerned about their mother's strange behaviour." The strain was such that at one point on the voyage, Diana disappeared for two hours, and after a widespread search of the yacht she was eventually located in one of the lifeboats, "crouched beneath the canvas cover in floods of tears".

It was only a matter of time until a formal announcement was made. Because the Prince of Wales is heir to the throne, the statement had to be made by the prime minister, John Major, in the House of Commons, and was not simply a terse palace press release such as those that marked the ending of the marriages of Princesses Margaret and Anne and the Duke of York. Diana asked that the statement should be released while the boys were still in the protected environment of Ludgrove and the date chosen was 9 December 1992. The week before, Diana drove to Ludgrove to explain the situation to the two boys. William, although only ten, took the news stoically and said, "I hope you will both be happy now." Diana knew from her own experience the long-term repercussions that separation and divorce can have on children, and she was concerned about the possible effect on William in particular. "He's a child that's a deep thinker and we won't know for a few years how it has gone in. But I put it gently without any resentment or anger."

Under the terms of the separation the boys would now divide their weekends away between Diana at Kensington Palace and Charles at Highgrove. The princess would drive to Ludgrove (and later to Eton College) to pick up the boys herself. At the palace they still occupied the nursery suite, where Diana had recently installed a wide-screen television for them, so they could watch the latest films on video or on satellite television. She tried to create the secure environment that was missing during her own childhood after her own parents parted in 1967 when she was only six. "I hug my children to death", she said shortly before the separation. "I get into bed with them at night, hug them and say, 'Who loves them most in the world?'

and they always say, 'Mummy'. I always feed them love and affection – it's so important." Diana clearly needed reassurance as much as she was desperate to give it.

This emotionally positive life of hugs and kisses was a radically new style of upbringing for royal children. Diana and Charles brought a warm style of parenting into a royal family that was more renowned for suppressing emotions than for expressing them. Lord Hurd, the former Conservative foreign secretary, who accompanied the Queen on several overseas tours, noted, "[the Queen] has almost trained feelings out of herself." One of her earlier private secretaries, Martin Charteris, agreed that the whole royal family "do feel things, but they don't feel very much". Self-control was a prerequisite of the role of royal prince or princess, but it came at a cost to the emotional lives of so many of them, particularly Prince Charles who, according to the writer Graham Turner, "has never been able to understand the apparent lack of maternal instinct in his mother".

While life for the boys at Kensington Palace continued much as it had before their parents' split, life at Highgrove was to change significantly. Not only were all signs of Diana's occupancy removed in a redecoration by the designer Robert Kime, but, more significantly, Charles appointed family friend Alexandra Legge-Bourke, whose mother Shan is a lady-in-waiting to their Aunt Anne, the Princess Royal, to act as a companion to the boys, someone who could look after them when Charles was away. She was nicknamed "Tiggy" after the Mrs Tiggywinkle's nursery school she worked for in London, and she is known for her great sense of humour, her boundless energy and her ability to relate well with children of all ages.

Tiggy was almost the same age as Diana. She had completed her education at the same finishing school, enjoyed swimming and tennis as much as Diana did and, like the princess, she had worked in a nursery school. Not surprisingly, Diana felt that her role was being usurped and

Overleaf: A touching moment as Diana arrives on board the Royal Yacht Britannia to greet her sons during a tour of Canada in October 1991. The boys, enjoying a half-term holiday, arrived the day before their parents. It was the first time both boys had accompanied their parents during an official visit.

Below: In 1992 Diana predicted that "William is going to be in his position much earlier than people think now". She was determined to prepare him for his future role as king and to ensure that Harry would always be there to help him.

went as far as telling friends such as Elsa Bowker that she was sure that Buckingham Palace had hired Tiggy in order to brainwash her sons so that they would be weaned away from her. For her part Tiggy was unconcerned about being in the firing line in the disputes between Charles and Diana, telling Patrick Jephson, "Doesn't bother me, I'm just the nursery maid, guv."

Although Charles and Diana were in opposing camps, Diana was very keen that William should respect his royal heritage. She maintained a warm relationship with the Queen even after the separation, and she once said, "It's very important to me that my sons have a very good relationship with the Queen." She was also surprisingly loyal to the Prince of Wales and hated any criticism of him by third parties. "The princess never liked that sort of thing and would rebuke them saying, 'Remember that he's the father of my children'", said her friend Roberto Devorik, the fashion entrepreneur.

Above: William has inherited his mother's love of swimming and tennis. Here the two are clearly thrilled by the action on Wimbledon's centre court during the 1991 tournament.

Diana also began to introduce William to royal duties at an early age. In 1987 when he was only five, Diana was asked to launch the National Hospital's £9.5 million appeal fund. Later, having been sent a video of the event, she replied by letter, "I made William sit down and look at it with me – I thought it was time that he should see this sort of thing – and we were both fascinated."

In those early days both William and Harry made appearances at official receptions held at Kensington Palace and Highgrove, staying for just a few minutes to be introduced to guests before quietly disappearing off to the nursery. Their good manners were also apparent in the many thank-you notes that Diana taught them to write, as she made clear in a comment when William was only ten. "If I come back from a dinner party or somewhere that needs a letter at midnight, I'll sit down and write it there and not wait until next morning because it would wrestle with my conscience. And now William does it – it's great."

Diana was also keen to groom William into a less traditional path of royal service since, as a friend of hers pointed out to Andrew Morton, "She believes that the (royal) family won't know what has hit it in a few years' time unless it changes too." When William was only nine, Diana took him to visit her friend Adrian Ward-Jackson who was dying from an AIDS-related illness. Adrian was being cared for by his friend Angela Serota, a former dancer with the Royal Ballet, who later recalled that William "had a mature view of illness, a perspective which showed awareness of love and commitment". William had brought with him a present of a large jasmine plant grown in the hothouses at Highgrove. On the way home he asked Diana, "If Adrian starts to die when I'm at school will you tell me so that I can be there?"

In the five years between the breakdown of the marriage and Diana's death, the princess took William to hostels and night shelters for the homeless. Cardinal Basil Hume, then head of the Catholic Church in England, joined them on a

Right: Alexandra "Tiggy" Legge-Bourke readily took on the role of friend and companion to the two princes. Here in October 1995 the three of them shop for fireworks in Tetbury High Street, near to the Highgrove estate.

visit to the Passage Day Centre for the homeless and told Diana that William "has such dignity at such a young age". Diana later took Harry on these visits too and commented, "They have a knowledge. They may never use it, but the seed is there, and I hope that it will grow because knowledge is power. I want them to have an understanding of people's emotions, people's insecurities, people's distress and people's hopes and dreams."

Part of the success of the visits to night shelters and hostels was that they were low key and without the formalities and restraints of a traditional royal visit. Diana encouraged the same type of informality in the boys' free time as well. Previous generations of the royal family had mixed solely within the higher echelons of society; their playmates and best friends were either siblings, cousins or the children of courtiers. William and Harry were encouraged to play with the Burrell children and those of other members of staff. Diana took them to McDonald's in Kensington or farther into town to the Hard Rock Café. Later there were visits to Thorpe Park, the theme park just to the west of London, and to the white-knuckle rides at Alton Towers in Staffordshire. There were visits to Disney World in Florida, to

Above: Following the break-up of the royal marriage, Diana organized activities for the boys that were far removed from the country pursuits so loved by the royal family. Staying at film star Goldie Hawn's ranch near Aspen, Colorado, Diana and her sons were seen enjoying white water rafting on the appropriately named Roaring Fork River.

the Rocky Mountains and to the Caribbean, all of which received coverage in the newspapers, and all of which Charles's camp regarded as publicity stunts on the part of the princess.

The holidays gave William and Harry a much-needed respite from the increasingly fraught atmosphere between their parents. The conflict reached its lowest point in the mid-1990s, just as William was reaching his teenage years. In a television interview in June 1994 with the broadcaster Jonathan Dimbleby, Charles admitted his adultery with Camilla Parker Bowles. In November of 1995 Diana admitted that she had had an affair with a Life Guards officer called James Hewitt. "Yes, I adored him. Yes, I was in love with him", she told her interviewer Martin Bashir before adding, "I was very let down." The most damaging confession was not about adultery but about Diana's firm conviction that Charles would never gain what she called the "top job" and that the throne would pass directly to William after the eventual death of the Queen.

William was at Eton College at the time of Diana's *Panorama* interview and opted to watch the one-hour programme alone in his housemaster's study. Although he was shielded from newspaper and further television coverage as much as possible, it would have been impossible for him to be protected totally from the one topic that dominated the tabloids nearly every day. The Queen, gravely concerned about the effect of the interview on her grandsons and on the future of the monarchy, immediately wrote to both Charles and Diana urging them to consider an early divorce as the sad but inevitable next move. Divorce proceedings began in February and the divorce was finalized on 28 August 1996. Custody of William and Harry was to be shared equally between Charles and Diana, with the prince becoming financially responsible for his sons' education, holidays, clothes and medical needs.

During the legal wrangling, it became apparent that Diana would lose the courtesy title of Her Royal Highness (HRH), which had been bestowed on her automatically on the day of her marriage. It was this, rather than the divorce, that formally signified her expulsion from the royal

Below: Wearing blue oilskins to protect them from the spray, Diana, Harry and the nine-year-old William are on board the tour boat 'Maid of the Mist' to experience a close-up view of Niagara Falls on the border between the United States and Canada. They admired the falls from the Canadian side.

family. When she told William the news he hugged her and said, "I don't care what you're called. You're Mummy."

During this final phase of Diana's life, William began to emerge as his mother's confidant and protector in a role-reversal that was more than apparent to those who were close to the princess. Rosa Monckton recalled that Diana "told [him] more things than most mothers would have told their children." Roberto Devorik was told by the princess that she had many profound conversations with her eldest son and that he was a great moral support.

Even before his parents separated William was trying his best to console Diana. After one family row the princess locked herself away in the bathroom to recover, and William pushed tissues under the door with a note saying, "Don't cry". On another occasion when Diana was distressed, William phoned her favourite restaurant, San Lorenzo, to book a table for the two of them. Diana's brother Charles noted how William was developing into a thoughtful and mature teenager. "William is a very self-possessed, intelligent and mature boy and quite shy. He is quite formal and stiff, sounding older than his years when he answers the phone."

Diana publicly acknowledged William's support in the summer of 1997, when at his instigation she auctioned seventy-nine of her designer outfits in New York in what was regarded by many as a farewell to her old life as a working royal. The auction raised $3.2 million for cancer and AIDS charities and Diana revealed, "It was all down to William, it was his idea."

Three weeks later, on 11 July 1997, a helicopter landed in the grounds of Kensington Palace to take Diana, William and Harry on their last holiday together. On board were their host Mohamed Al Fayed, the Egyptian-born owner of Harrods International, his wife Heini and their four children. The party flew to Nice, where they boarded the Al Fayed yacht *Jonikal* and headed for St Tropez where the family owns a villa. Two days into the holiday they were joined by Dodi Al Fayed, Mohamed's forty-two-year-old son from his first marriage. The holiday ended abruptly on 20 July when Diana heard of the death of her friend, the designer Gianni Versace, who had been shot outside his Miami Beach mansion. Diana immediately returned to London to prepare for the funeral, but before leaving St Tropez she arranged to return to the villa with Dodi in early August.

Above: September 1995 and nearly three years after formally separating, Diana and Charles put on a show of unity for William's first day at Eton. Joined by housemaster Dr Jonathan Gailey, the family pose outside Manor House, which would be William's home for the next five years.

On the night of 30 August 1997 Diana dined with Dodi at another Al Fayed property, the Paris Ritz. Shortly after arriving at the Ritz, Diana received a call from an anxious William who had been asked by the Buckingham Palace press office to agree to a photocall to mark the start of his third term at Eton. The idea was to allow the press occasional access in return for privacy during the rest of the academic year. William, however, was concerned that focusing attention on him would overshadow Harry, a concern that Diana shared.

While the prince went to bed at Balmoral, Diana ate with Dodi in their rooms at the hotel. Shortly after midnight they left to return to his Paris home a few minutes' drive away. While their Mercedes drove at speed through the deserted streets, at least six photographers tore after them on

motorcycles, trying to capture the princess for yet another photograph. As the car hurtled towards the place de l'Alma, the chauffeur lost control of the vehicle, sending it spinning uncontrollably into one of the concrete pillars that supported the tunnel de pont de l'Alma.

Both Prince Charles and the Queen were woken in the early hours of the morning when news of the accident was forwarded from Paris to Buckingham Palace and then on to Balmoral. The prince decided to let his sons sleep on until 7.30 when they normally awoke. Fifteen minutes later he went to their adjoining rooms to break the news to them that their mother was dead.

Above: Diana clearly adored both her sons. "I know we had two boys for a reason. We were the only people in the family to have two boys. The rest of the family had a boy and a girl and we were the first to change and I know fate played a hand there."

The following week would see the Queen and her family attacked from all quarters for the way they conducted themselves in the immediate aftermath. They were criticized for being cold and remote and for not responding to the near-hysterical reaction that developed during the following days. There was of course no criticism of William and Harry, who conducted themselves with remarkable control and showed maturity far beyond their years.

Less than four hours after hearing of Diana's death, the boys ran the gauntlet of photographers when they attended the normal Sunday morning service at nearby Crathie kirk. Later in the week they were photographed examining bouquets of flowers left outside the entrance to the Balmoral estate. The following day they again managed to remain composed as they took flowers from well-wishers in the grounds of their mother's Kensington Palace home, while a few miles away their grandmother paid a television tribute to Diana praising "her energy and commitment to others, especially her two boys".

The following day William and Harry stood alongside their father, their uncle Earl Spencer and Prince Philip as Diana's cortège slowly moved into view along The Mall. Under the gaze of thousands of onlookers and millions of television viewers, the boys walked behind their mother's coffin as it made its farewell journey through the capital.

Below: Diana ensured that William had as normal an upbringing as possible. In March 1995 they joined other rugby fans on the London to Cardiff InterCity rail service to watch the England-Wales rugby international.

Diana once said that William and Harry were the only two men who had never let her down, and in the years following her death they have continued to protect her memory. In those years everyone from lovers and friends to hairdressers and therapists has jumped on the very lucrative bandwagon. William felt compelled to criticize the memoirs of Diana's former private secretary Patrick Jephson as a "betrayal". He was similarly critical of the memoirs of Ken Wharfe, her last protection officer, and he revealed that he was "sickened" by a planned film of her life using tape recordings she made in the early 1990s.

William was also concerned that the reaction after Diana's death was constantly being fanned by the press and

television even months later. On the first anniversary, and on his own initiative, William asked for a statement to be released in which both he and Harry thanked people for mourning Diana, and for offering sympathy, but suggesting that it was now time to move on and to look forwards rather than backwards.

That statement was a sign of William's growing maturity and self-reliance, which have become more apparent since Diana's death. He has her looks, her hair, her mannerisms, her habit of blushing easily and her infectious laugh, but he has inherited far more. He is compassionate and a skilled communicator with people from all walks of life. He has her social conscience and her belief that royalty can no longer exist in the imperial style of splendour into which his father and grandmother were born. More significantly, he has her strong, independent streak. While he respects his royal heritage he is not afraid to challenge its conventions. This will ensure that Diana's legacy will continue far into this century and perhaps beyond.

Left: William and Harry remained unbelievably composed as, flanked by their father, their uncle Earl Spencer and their grandfather Prince Philip, they followed their mother's funeral cortège on its slow progress to Westminster Abbey.

Right: A stunned William gazes at some of the millions of floral tributes laid in memory of Diana outside Kensington Palace. Later Charles revealed that he was "unbelievably proud" of the way his sons "have handled a very difficult time with enormous courage and the greatest possible dignity".

Left: William steals a glance at the hearse carrying his mother's body as Diana leaves London for the final time, heading for her childhood home of Althorp House in Northamptonshire.

CHAPTER TWO

WILLIAM AND CHARLES

W illiam's closeness to Diana was undeniable and never varied even in his adolescent years. The princess and her sons appeared in countless photographs hugging and kissing and enjoying fun days out at amusement parks or holidays in the Caribbean, and the public perception was of a close-knit bond between mother and sons. At the time the same couldn't be said of Charles and the boys. The press portrayed him as a remote father, who put duty and his love of polo before his love for his sons. When Charles took the boys to amusement parks he must have been the only father there wearing a suit with an over-coat, and photographs of William and Harry at royal occasions always showed them dressed in suits. The angle portrayed by the media, particu-larly in the late 1980s and early 1990s, was that Charles had failed as a father. His concern for the boys in the aftermath of Diana's death and their evident ease in their relationship with him has proved beyond doubt that that is not true.

Charles's image as a formal and emotionally detached father derives not only from the contrast he made with the more tactile and unreserved Diana, but is also in part because of his own relationship with his parents. Charles was a very shy and insecure child and, as his official biographer Jonathan Dimbleby points out, the

prince's "relationship with his parents has never been easy: the gulf of misunderstanding that often exists between the generations has been sharpened by the intense pressures of public life, and the expression of mutual affection doesn't come easily to any of them." As a child Charles was said to have been frightened of Prince Philip who, according to some courtiers, "did rather jump down his throat", whereas the Queen "was not indifferent so much as detached, deciding that in domestic matters she would submit entirely to the father's will".

Charles was hoping to find fulfilment and security in family life and, like Diana, he wanted children, not just for dynastic reasons, but also to complete the family unit. An hour after William's birth, Charles emerged to a rapturous welcome from the crowds, who greeted him with a rendition of "For He's A Jolly Good Fellow", and many of whom tried to grab his hand or kiss him. As he was jostled towards the press, a newsman shouted, "Is he like you, sir?" Charles still grinning with delight said, "No, fortunately", before adding that witnessing his son's birth was an overwhelming experience, "a very adult thing to do". In a letter to his friends the van Cutsems, Charles wrote, "I got back here just before midnight – utterly elated but quite shattered. I can't tell you how excited and proud I am." Another letter, written a few days later to his godmother, Countess Mountbatten, found Charles still mesmerized by the whole experience. "The arrival of our small son has been an astonishing experience and one that has meant more to me than I ever could have imagined ... I am *so* thankful I was beside Diana's bedside the whole time because by the end of the day I really felt as though I'd shared deeply in the process of birth and as a result was rewarded by seeing a small creature which belonged to *us* even though he seemed to belong to everyone else as well!"

Above: Looking like any other father and son, Charles and William arrive at Aberdeen Airport for a family holiday in August 1984. Only the crown and granny's cipher on the aircraft of the Queen's Flight give the game away.

Emerging from the hospital the following day, it was Charles who carried his tiny son to the car. Earlier, the baby's grandfather Earl Spencer had told the assembled journalists that Charles was "absolutely over the moon". Even in the acrimonious run-up to their separation, Diana recalled those early days with affection and still praised Charles's attitude: "He loved the nursery life and couldn't wait to get back and do the bottle and everything. He was very good, he always came back and fed the baby ...."

This bond with children was evident even before the birth of William. His first private secretary, Sir David Checketts, recalled that Charles "was wonderful with our kids", even as a teenager. "At one point our son Simon had whooping cough and once woke Leila and myself in the middle of the night. When we went into his room, we found Prince Charles already there trying to make him more comfortable."

For a man unaccustomed to cuddling and kissing babies, Charles made a great effort to be a "hands-on" father, slowly becoming more tactile with his son, and was even known to change the occasional nappy. Earl Spencer, who as a former equerry to the Queen had known Charles since he was a small boy, commented, "The fact that (Charles and Diana) refuse to be separated from William, unless it is really necessary, is quite different from what even Prince Charles experienced."

Charles was fascinated by each stage of his son's development. In a letter to his mother's lady-in-waiting, Lady Susan Hussey, the besotted father wrote, "I must tell you that your godson couldn't be in better form. He looks horribly well and is expanding visibly and with frightening rapidity. Today he actually crawled for the first time. We laughed and laughed with sheer, hysterical pleasure and now we can't stop him crawling everywhere." To reciprocate the admiration, Diana arranged for a card to be sent to Charles on the first Father's Day after William's birth, when the couple were on a tour of Canada. The front of it showed a magician pulling a rabbit out of a hat, and the message inside said, "Dad I think you're magic".

The affectionate bond between father and son continued despite Charles's absence on public duties and overseas tours. William was always excited to see his father and would rush out to see the red Wessex helicopters of the Queen's Flight land on the parkland at Highgrove or at

Right: William and Charles on board the Royal Yacht Britannia during the Waleses' visit to Venice in May 1985. If occasionally royal tours coincided with school holidays, Charles and Diana would take the boys with them. Frustratingly for the locals the young princes stayed aboard the yacht and rarely appeared at official royal functions.

Kensington Palace. William then hurled himself at his father, regardless of how muddy the grass was, and Charles would joke, "the number of times I've had to go and get changed the minute I arrive home".

By the mid-1980s the Waleses' marriage was in difficulty and William was by then old enough to be aware of the tense atmosphere, the rows and the unexpected departure of either or both parents. By 1987 Charles had moved out of Kensington Palace and taken apartments at St James's Palace just along The Mall from Buckingham Palace. William and Harry would spend the week with their mother and would then travel down to Highgrove for weekends with Charles.

Charles now saw less of the boys than he would have liked. Diana wanted to ease herself away from the rigid world of royal protocol and formality and to let her sons experience as normal an upbringing as possible. As relations between the couple deteriorated their respective private secretaries took on the additional duty of trying to ensure that both parents received adequate access to the children. According to Jonathan Dimbleby, Charles's secretary Richard Aylard sent a memo to his boss asking whether Charles would be able to negotiate "windows" for an outing with the children or whether he would like the staff to negotiate for him. Charles, "in what appears to be an allusion to the difficulty of accommodating his diary to that of the Princess' scrawled in capital letters on the memo 'I'LL TRY!'"

The disputes had little impact on Charles's relationship with his two sons. A member of his household said later, "The prince always had a great time with his sons when they were together. The problem was they weren't together as often as he would have liked." What did have an impact on Charles was the popular perception that he was a remote father figure. "Before long", writes Dimbleby in Charles's biography, "the belief that the prince was, at best, a poor father, began to seep into an already poisoned public consciousness."

Left: Posing on the stone-walled patio in the gardens of Highgrove House in the summer of 1988. Six-year-old William and four-year-old Harry have little idea that their parents' marriage is under strain and that Diana would rarely visit the Gloucestershire mansion after this time.

Although the prince was often wrapped up in his work, he never in any way abandoned his sons or put their interests second, as many newspapers suggested. William and Harry's detective Ken Wharfe recently negated another myth surrounding Charles and the boys. In his memoirs Wharfe wrote, "Much has been made in the press about the relationship between the prince, and their protection officers, often with exaggerated claims that they regarded 'their' policemen as some form of surrogate father. This of course was nonsense. To William and Harry the Prince of Wales was always 'Papa', and nobody could or would ever take his place." Wharfe went on, "It was not that he was not a good father, despite the black propaganda circulated abut him at the time, it was just that he found the kind of horseplay that his boys sometimes needed at that stage in their lives somewhat confusing." In spite of the "confusion", Charles did take part in some of the rough and tumble of nursery life and one of the young princes' favourite games was "Big Bad Wolf", in which Charles – as the wolf – tried to stop them escaping his clutches as they ran riot in the nursery.

The boys spent their weekends at Highgrove, Charles's estate, set in 348 acres of parkland on the edge of the Cotswolds. Here William could ride around the estate on his bike, skateboard along the paths and ride his Shetland pony away from the prying eyes of journalists and photographers. There were also a climbing frame, a tree house and a swimming pool and, more importantly, his cousins Peter and Zara, the Princess Royal's two children, lived at Gatcombe Park, just ten kilometres (six miles) away.

William grew accustomed to country pursuits from an early age and was happy to accompany Charles when he was shooting at Sandringham or stalking at Balmoral. By the time of Diana's death William was as comfortable with the hunting, shooting and fishing world of his royal relations as he was with the activities he shared with his mother. Charles with his depth of knowledge on country issues was keen to pass on his love of the environment to his eldest son, and was particularly pleased that William would respond with a stream of questions that showed he had a genuine interest in the same areas.

Just as Prince Philip and his uncle, Earl Mountbatten, had encouraged Charles to take up polo, so Charles in turn arranged for William to have

Right: 16 August 1997 and the three princes pose for a relaxed family shot on the banks of the River Dee on the Queen's Balmoral estate. No one could have predicted that exactly two weeks later, Diana's life would reach its tragic end.

lessons. Charles gave William a polo pony as a seventeenth birthday present and he stabled it at Fort Belvedere in Windsor Great Park.

According to Dimbleby, Charles "hoped to influence his children towards sharing a growing number of his own tastes", and so, besides sport, he was also keen to share with them his great love of painting, music and the theatre. When William and Harry were old enough he regularly took them to see the Royal Shakespeare Company at Stratford-upon-Avon.

Their shared enthusiasms helped to change the dynamics of the father-son relationship, bringing William and Charles closer than they had ever been. Courtiers told the writer Graham Turner, "In the years before his parents' separation, Prince William had sometimes expressed anger with his father because he so often seemed to upset his mother. As the years went by, however, he began to feel much more at home with Charles, partly because they shared the same enthusiasms."

A defining moment of the relationship proved to be a skiing holiday at Klosters during William's spring half term in 1994. Sixty photographers arrived at the Swiss ski resort keen to document the contrast in style between the formality of a holiday with Charles and the more relaxed breaks that Diana always managed to create. Journalists were ready to report that the holiday was a disaster and the boys were bored and ill at ease. Instead Charles made sure his sons had a great time. He invited the boys' fun-loving nanny Tiggy Legge-Bourke to join the royal party, which also included his friends the Palmer-Tompkinsons and their wildly extrovert daughter Tara. A clearly relaxed Charles was photographed hugging his sons, and in a Diana-type gesture he insisted the boys queue for ski lifts instead of being ushered ahead of other skiers. In order to stay with his sons Charles kept to the normal blue trails rather than skiing off-piste on the black runs. Later he joined them for après-ski sessions of bowling, tobogganing and swimming before dining in the hotel restaurant. The holiday went some way to prove to cynical newspapers and their generally pro-Diana readers that Charles was a sensitive and loving father after all.

The event that truly cemented their close relationship was the one event that no one could have predicted – Diana's death. With hindsight, it was fortunate that William and Harry happened to be staying with their father

Above: William has inherited his father's interest in the arts, the environment, architecture, country sports and, of course, polo. Charles played his first match in 1963 under the tutelage of Prince Philip and Earl Mountbatten, a top-class player who always competed as 'Marco'".

at Balmoral when the devastating news was relayed from Paris. Not only were William and Harry shielded from the media on the most private of the royal estates, but Charles was able to break the news to them himself, which wouldn't have been the case if the accident had happened a week later when William was back at Eton and Harry at Ludgrove.

From the moment the news was broken to the princes, the royal family and its courtiers floundered through a welter of protocol and precedent to decide on an appropriate way to mourn an ex-member of the family who, nevertheless, had been the mother of a future king. While for once the Queen appeared weak and vacillating, Charles remained uncharacteristi-

cally decisive. Despite advice to the contrary, he made immediate plans to fly to Paris to bring his former wife's body home. Diana may have been stripped of her HRH status the previous year but he insisted that a royal standard – to which she was technically not entitled – should cover the plain coffin. Diana's remains were returned in an aircraft of the Queen's Flight and received at RAF Northolt in north-west London with full military honours. Charles insisted that the hearse should be escorted to London by a team of police outriders, who would normally escort the royal family on public engagements. Charles's concern that Diana should receive all the trappings and honour that befit a princess and his decision to take control

Above: With the stunning landscape of the Swiss Alps as a backdrop, Charles and William take a ski lift to the slopes above Klosters the resort Charles has visited nearly every year since 1977. Diana preferred to take her sons to the Austrian resort of Lech.

WILLIAM AND CHARLES

of many aspects of the funeral arrangements gained him the lasting respect of William and brought father and son closer than ever before.

While the young princes remained at Balmoral, Charles arranged for Tiggy Legge-Bourke to fly to Aberdeen to join them, thereby ensuring that alongside the habitual stiff-upper-lip attitude of the Queen and her household, there was someone there who could cuddle the boys and who could cry and laugh, go for walks and swim with them, and be there for them whenever they needed to talk to someone.

In the months following Diana's death the royal family made a determined effort to regain the respect that had been lost in the immediate aftermath, when the Queen and her family were criticized for appearing to be unfeeling and trapped in a world of protocol. The Queen herself acknowledged this three months later in a speech to mark her golden wedding, when she admitted that it was often difficult to assess the public's thinking, "obscured as it can be by deference, rhetoric or the conflicting currents of public opinion".

Below: 29 March 2002 and the three princes pose for the now obligatory photocall at the start of their Easter holiday in Klosters. The following afternoon news reached them of the death of Charles's beloved grandmother, the Queen Mother. All three princes were said to be "utterly devastated" and William and Harry did their best to console their grieving father.

WILLIAM

Above: A Buckingham Palace balcony appearance to mark the Queen Mother's 100th birthday on 4 August 2000. William, by now, is far more at ease in public,

Left: June 1999 and William at 6ft 2in towers over his father and brother. The princes pose outside the main entrance to the Highgrove estate to mark William's seventeenth birthday.

The death of the princess returned Charles to the centre stage of royal life. Without the constant rivalry that had existed between his camp and Diana's, Charles gained confidence noticeably. The public in general was sympathetic to his efforts to bring up his two sons alone. He restructured his work and leisure time so that his world could revolve around the needs of his sons. His biographer Anthony Holden commented soon after Diana's death that "By cancelling engagements to be with his sons, Charles was earning far greater popularity than he could ever have done by carrying them out".

After a family Christmas at Sandringham, Charles took the boys to Klosters for a week's skiing. In the spring of 1998, after announcing that he would be "streamlining" his charities so that he could spend more time with his sons, Charles took Prince Harry on safari in South Africa and for a very public meeting with the Spice Girls in Cape Town. In March he took the boys on a semi-public visit to British Columbia, where he was delighted by William's rapturous reception by thousands of Vancouver's teenagers.

In another sensitive gesture he asked interior designer Robert Kime to recreate the boys' Kensington Palace suite of rooms as closely as possible in an apartment at St James's Palace. After their mother's death William and Harry did not want to spend another night at their mother's home. Charles arranged for them to take over York House, a self-contained five-bedroomed apartment within St James's but with a separate entrance, which had until recently been used by the Duke and Duchess of Kent. Five months after Diana's death the boys made a poignant tour of their old home to choose keepsakes and to decide which items of furniture they would like relocated. They selected the giant television that Diana had bought for them and, ignoring the priceless antiques and paintings, they chose to take the collection of cuddly toys that Diana always kept in her bedroom. Realizing that William was reaching the stage when he would want more independence, Charles gave him a key to his York House flat so that he could come and go as he pleased and so that he could bring friends from Eton back for weekend "stopovers" after nights out in London's West End.

Charles has been keen to make sure that each rite of passage since Diana's death is marked in an appropriate way. When William passed his driving test in the summer of 1999, his father bought him a VW Golf as a seventeenth birthday present. Although less happy with William's choice of a motorbike for his eighteenth birthday, he bought him a 125cc Kawasaki and William practised on it at Highgrove. In 2002, two years after completing the basic test, William passed his motorcycle test. Charles, like any father, was concerned that his son would want to upgrade to a larger and faster machine. One consolation for him is that William has proved to be a competent and sensible driver. After passing his driving test at the first attempt he went on to take and pass the advanced Pass Plus scheme.

Like any single parent, Charles has found that the responsibility of bringing up two sons can be stressful even though their lives are cushioned by financial security and the luxury of a staff of dozens. The prince told royal biographer Ingrid Seward, "I worry so much for them", and on occasions his anxiety has been justified. In August 1998, barely a year after Diana's death, the prince was horrified to learn that William and Harry had abseiled down the 48-metre (156-foot) Grwyne-Fawr dam in Monmouthshire without safety helmets, second lines or the permission of Welsh Water, the company that operates the reservoir. Charles was greatly concerned about the incident and asked for a detailed report from those present, including Tiggy Legge-Bourke and the boys' detectives.

Another worry for Charles was how to integrate his life with his sons with his life with Camilla Parker Bowles. In a 1994 BBC documentary to

mark his first twenty-five years as Prince of Wales, Charles admitted to
Jonathan Dimbleby that he had been faithful in his marriage to Diana,
"until it became irretrievably broken down, us both having tried". He also
admitted that Mrs Parker Bowles had been "the mainstay" of his life for
many years. Off-camera he confirmed to Dimbleby that the marriage had
broken down in 1986 immediately upon his resumption of his relationship
with Camilla.

While Diana was alive, William had no intention of meeting Camilla.
After the princess's death there was an uneasy juggling of diaries and itin-
eraries to ensure that the two parties never met. Camilla stayed at her own
Gloucestershire home whenever William and Harry were at Highgrove
and avoided her rooms at St James's Palace when the boys were in London.

The first recorded meeting between William and Camilla occurred at
St James's Palace on 12 June 1998, nine days before William's sixteenth
birthday. The prince had apparently called into the palace for a change of
clothes before a cinema trip with friends. Mrs Parker Bowles happened to
be there at the time, and although Charles gave his son the option of *not*
meeting Camilla, William declined it and went in for what was described
later as a "cordial and general discussion about all manner of things".
Afterwards, a clearly relieved Camilla asked for a strong vodka and tonic

Left: Camilla Parker
Bowles has been
gradually integrated into
William's life and is now a
familiar figure at Prince
Charles' Highgrove estate.

to calm her nerves. The two met shortly afterwards for tea, and at a lunch party a few weeks later William sat opposite Mrs Parker Bowles. This pattern of events was carefully leaked to the press in July as part of the ongoing process of gaining public acceptance for Camilla after Diana's death. If the princess's sons approved of the relationship then it would be all the more difficult for the public to ostracize Camilla.

The meeting between William and Camilla came at a good time, just a few months before Charles's fiftieth birthday. William was organizing a surprise party for his father and it would have been very difficult to invite over a hundred of Charles's friends, relations and associates but not invite the most important woman in his life. Although his birthday was on 14 November, the party was held at Highgrove at the end of July to accommodate royal engagements and school commitments. The highlight was a comedy play produced by Oscar-winning actress Emma Thompson and comedian Stephen Fry, in which both William and Harry took part.

In January 1999, Charles and Camilla were photographed together in public for the first time in a quarter of a century when they left a private party at London's Ritz Hotel. The next significant step was for Camilla to be photographed at a public event attended by both William and Charles. The chosen event was a reception in February 2001 to mark the tenth anniversary of the Press Complaints Commission. The PCC had been formed with the co-operation of every major British newspaper as a voluntary watchdog for the industry, and as every newspaper editor was present at the reception, some of them compared the event to throwing three nervous Christians into the lion's den.

By this time William and Harry had become friends with Camilla's two children Laura and Tom. Charles, Camilla and their four children enjoyed a holiday cruise around the Greek islands in the summer of 1999 and in the same year William was spotted with Tom at London's K-Bar in Soho. The two became regulars at the Chelsea restaurant Foxtrot Oscar and have also spent weekends at Highgrove with Prince Harry, Laura and their parents.

In May 1999, Tom was caught offering cocaine to an undercover reporter while he was working for a PR company in Cannes. After the story broke he was forced to return home and he resigned from his job. While Charles regretted the fact that Tom, one of his godsons, hit the headlines only because of his mother's relationship with the prince, he was also concerned about the possible knock-on effect on William who regarded Tom as an older brother figure. In a show of solidarity Charles's office released a statement. "Prince Charles and Mrs Parker Bowles are primarily concerned with the welfare of all the children – William, Harry, Tom and Laura. They are all part of the extended family. An open mind is kept about all methods of support and all routes of help that are available." Privately Charles discussed the perils of drug addiction with his eldest son and William promised to avoid the temptation that so many in his social circle – including his distant cousin Lord Frederick Windsor – have given in to.

Although William will always be associated closely with his mother because of his looks, his mannerisms and his soft, natural voice, as well as the ease with which he communicates with people, there are also strong similarities to Charles – from his controlled personality, which enables him to hide his real feelings in public, to his interests in art and the environment. According to one of Charles's friends, William "is a chip off his father's block. When they are together there is an enormous sense of fun ... there is always a lot of ragging." The relaxed warmth is evident at the annual photocall on the ski slopes of Klosters when William and Harry show no embarrassment about posing with their arms around Charles's shoulders. The easy rapport was also noticeable when Charles invited journalists to Highgrove prior to William's trip to Chile during his year off from university. When William said that his father had helped "slightly" to raise the money for the trip, Charles joked, "I chip in all the bloody time!" Similarly, when father and son undertook a day of engagements in Scotland in September 2001, William was heard to say, "I have never been propositioned so much in all my life. But my Dad's the real babe magnet."

It is all so different from the formality that characterized Charles's relationship with his parents. Newsreels from the early 1950s show the Queen returning from an overseas tour and shaking hands formally with her small son who looks bewildered by the plethora of officials, cameramen and applauding onlookers. We have go back a century to discover a similarly warm relationship between a future king and his son. After Edward VII's

Right: Although Charles has found increasing fulfilment in his public role in recent years, his proudest role is as a father. William's emergence as a diligent, thoughtful and sensitive personality is a tribute to both of them as well as to the legacy of Diana.

death in 1910, his son, the future George V, wrote in a diary entry, "I have lost my best friend and the best of fathers. I never had a [cross] word with him in my life. I am heartbroken and overwhelmed with grief."

The fact that William and Charles have managed to forge a strong and loving relationship after the traumatic years of William's youth is a tribute to the strength of character that both men possess.

CHAPTER THREE

WILLIAM AND HARRY

If William is in the unenviable position of being the man "born to be king", Prince Harry is even less fortunate in being the "spare" to his brother's "heir". Lacking any formal role in the British constitution, Harry is nevertheless as trapped in the British monarchy as William is, since historically there is a significant possibility that Harry could one day become Henry IX. In the twentieth century two second sons succeeded to the throne. The Queen's father Albert, Duke of York, became George VI following his brother's abdication, and their father George V had also expected to remain Duke of York until the death of his elder brother, the Duke of Clarence pushed him into direct succession.

Prince Charles's vision of a slimmed-down monarchy to counter public criticism of the so-called "hangers-on", will again focus more attention on William and Harry as their uncles, aunts and cousins gradually withdraw into the background. Princess Margaret once remarked, "In my own sort of humble way I have always tried to take some part of the burden from my sister. She can't do it all." Harry's role will likewise be to support his brother by shouldering the burden of royal engagements and being present at key events on the royal calendar from Trooping the Colour to hosting state visits. He will be expected to act as a Counsellor of

Right: Princes William and Harry leave St George's Chapel, Windsor, following the understated wedding of their uncle Prince Edward to Sophie Rhys-Jones on 19 June 1999.

Left: Five-year-old William offers a guiding hand as Harry, aged three, arrives for his first day at Mrs Mynor's nursery school in west London's Notting Hill in 1987.

State whenever William is out of the country and he will be patron or president of a host of charities.

What will make Harry's task easier is the strong relationship that exists between the two brothers. Born just two years apart, William and Harry have relied on each other for support and friendship in the rarefied atmosphere that inevitably surrounds royalty. Despite the brothers' different characters, there is an underlying trust and respect and a shared sense of humour that recalls the relationship between the Queen and Princess Margaret. The sensible elder sister was always protective of her younger rebellious sister. Margaret, like Harry, was the prankster who teased her often-solemn sister and who became the original royal rebel.

William and Harry have had to face their own pressures. For the first ten years of Harry's life, William was the self-appointed protector of his initially shy and reserved brother who was to follow in his footsteps from nanny to nursery school to prep school. In the years between Charles and Diana's separation in 1992 and their divorce nearly four years later William became less confident, found it virtually impossible to cope with the intrusion of press photographers and hated life in the public spotlight. Harry, like Margaret in the 1930s, blossomed in the public arena, waved cheekily out of car windows, posed happily for the photocalls on the annual skiing holidays and teased his often morose sibling.

Prince Henry Charles Albert David of Wales entered the world at 4.20 p.m. on Saturday 15 September 1984. Shortly afterwards Buckingham Palace announced that the new prince would be known as Prince Harry, a name that was probably inspired by Charles's favourite Shakespearean character Henry V, hero of the Battle of Agincourt, whose renowned call to arms in the play *Henry V*, was the resounding "Cry 'God for Harry, England, and St George'."

Left: An early love of the countryside. William and Harry spent most weekends at Highgrove, the Waleses' Gloucestershire mansion. Here, dressed in Barbour jackets and Wellington boots, they spend a rainy day watching their father play polo at Cirencester.

According to Diana, the summer of 1984 when she was expecting Harry was when she and Charles were at their closest. Once again the couple read books on childcare and were conscious of the fact that the headstrong two-year-old William might find it difficult to adjust to a new face in the royal nursery. The morning after the birth William was brought to the Lindo Wing of St Mary's Hospital, Paddington, to meet his new brother and to try to forge a bond at the earliest opportunity. Diana decided to meet him at the door of the room and held him in her arms as she introduced the new baby to her first-born. William was affectionate from the beginning, wanting to hold Harry and to play with him. Any fears of jealousy were dispelled and Diana was clearly besotted with both boys, as she revealed in a letter to a friend at the time. "The reaction to his birth has totally over-

Right: "Wish you were here!" A thoughtful William and Harry pose for the cameras when the Waleses arrive to holiday with the Spanish royal family in Majorca in August 1987.

Left: October 1991, and the two denim-clad princes tour the Canadian frigate HMCS Ottawa on Lake Ontario while their parents were on an official tour of Canada.

whelmed us and we can hardly breathe for the masses of flowers that have arrived. William adores his little brother and spends the entire time pouring an endless supply of hugs and kisses on Harry, and we are hardly allowed near. I can't believe I am now a mother of two."

These were the early days of William's "Basher Billy" phase and, unfortunately for his parents, he chose Harry's christening to demonstrate just how to sabotage a dignified ceremony. During the photo session after the baptism the Queen tried to quieten William by getting him to play with the corgis, but he decided he'd much rather play with his three-year-old cousin Zara Phillips and chased her round the room instead.

Harry followed William to Mrs Mynor's nursery school in Notting Hill Gate in west London. "It made me feel very sad – I had a big lump in my throat when we left Harry", Charles revealed after his younger son's first day at school. Harry in those days was the shy, withdrawn one, although later this would change completely and Diana was heard to say, "Harry's the naughty one, just like me."

Diana tried to bring the boys up as normally as possible. Her father, naturally biased, gave her full credit for the way they were developing as children. "They're very lucky to have Diana as a mother. They lead fairly normal lives really as Diana has lots of girlfriends of her own age, all of whom have children." The Earl also felt that his grandsons were polite and well mannered when they had to be. "They behave very well when they are on duty and when they're off duty, they're normal little boys. There's no sibling rivalry between them."

To introduce them to their public roles as early as possible both Charles and Diana allowed the princes to appear briefly at charity receptions held at either Kensington Palace or Highgrove. This was a practice that the Queen Mother had encouraged decades before with her two daughters and the Queen in turn encouraged all four of her children to do the same. It meant that from an early age William and Harry were used to shaking hands with strangers and making small talk.

Charles and Diana insisted that the boys were treated the same, so that William never received preferential treatment in front of Harry. Each boy was present when the other started a new school, a process that continued

Left: Looking ahead to their destiny. The two young men who carry the future of the monarchy on their shoulders.

right through until Harry started at Eton. Charles was also particularly keen that the boys should be photographed together, again to avoid an emphasis on William. Having just two children made this even more crucial, and again recalls the childhood of Princesses Elizabeth and Margaret. Because of paper-rationing during the war, the number of pages in newspapers were limited and occasionally in group photographs of the King and Queen with their children, Princess Margaret would be omitted simply to save space. The King asked editors to illustrate either both or neither of his daughters to avoid Margaret being left out.

As Harry grew he became renowned as the joker of the family. Earl Spencer recalled when neither boy could be found during a visit to his Althorp estate. While their worried detectives hurried down to the lake in case they had decided to play there, their grandfather found them hiding in the library. "If I can't find either of them, I'll know where to look," he said later. Hiding in the library was pretty tame sport in comparison to what Harry got up a few years later. At the age of seven he climbed on to the roof of Kensington Palace to pelt the police sentry with snowballs. Two years later, while the family was relaxing on Richard Branson's Caribbean island of Necker, Harry led William and a group of friends to a cliff edge where they bombarded the unsuspecting paparazzi who were in boats moored below them.

Right: August 1995 and an early lesson in royal duty. As the Queen takes the salute during a review of Second World War veterans to mark the fiftieth anniversary of Victory in Japan Day, Harry and William are deep in conversation.

Harry's sense of humour was always useful in deflecting some of the tensions to which William was prone, particularly after their parents' separation. After one outburst when William snapped that he would never want to be king, Harry joked, "If you don't want to be king, I'll be king." Harry was also adept at getting round his mother when he'd pushed the boundaries too far, cuddling up to her to curry favour as Princess Margaret had done with her mother half a century earlier. An eyewitness recalled that Margaret had "a sparkling sense of wit, an appreciation of the ludicrous. It was she who could always make her father laugh, even when he was angry with her."

A continual source of amusement for Harry is the "Wills-mania" that turns teenage girls into gibbering wrecks whenever William appears in public. During their visit to Vancouver in March 1998 hordes of banner-

Above: Another day of celebration as the princes descend the steps outside the west door of St Paul's Cathedral following a thanksgiving service held to mark the Queen Mother's hundredth birthday, June 2000.

waving, hysterical girls trailed after the royal party in the hope of seeing William, much to his embarrassment. "Go on, wave at that lot," Harry urged William, giving him a prod in the back. When William did go over to see them, there was always renewed shrieking, to Harry's delight. As a royal aide commented at the time, "Life isn't going to be dull with Harry around." Occasionally Harry pushes his luck too far, as when he once angered his older brother by stopping him half-way through a cross-country race to ask for his autograph, mimicking the sort of screaming admirer that is the bane of William's life.

Harry is now as tall as William and while the older prince has the looks and mannerisms of his mother, Harry has the fiery red hair of his maternal aunt Lady Sarah McCorquodale and her son George, Harry's exact contemporary. Harry was named one of the best-dressed "sharp shooters" in 2001 for the dark suit and lavender pin-striped shirt he wore at the church service to mark Prince Philip's eightieth birthday. Shortly after his eighteenth birthday he was crowned 2002's "most dateable stud" in *Tatler*. The society magazine's editor Geordie Greig commented that "Harry has suddenly emerged as the young royal who has just come of age and is naughty but nice ... there's a certain energy and irreverence, wit and fun about him." William, who had been number one in a previous list, failed to make the top ten and is thrilled that it is now Harry who is riding high in fashion and pin-up polls, while he is starting to slip down them and no longer makes as many headlines for his clothes or his looks.

The easy rapport between the brothers will make their future working relationship all the smoother. It was Diana's hope that William and Harry would in some way share the responsibility of monarchy when William succeeds to the throne. She told Tina Brown, editor of *The New Yorker*, that she was grooming Harry to be "a huge support to his brother. The boys will be properly prepared. I am making sure of this", adding, "I don't want them to suffer the way I did", a reference to the difficulties she had in adjusting to life as a working royal in the full glare of the media.

Diana's death brought the two brothers even closer together. In the years since her death the two princes have seen their mother's name and legacy constantly battered by a series of books and magazine exclusives by seemingly everyone who had contact with her. After William's pointed comments about the memoirs of her private secretary Patrick Jephson, Harry in turn defended her name in an interview to mark his eighteenth birthday when he said, in an oblique reference to Ken Wharfe's book, "The fifth anniversary of her death was important because she wasn't remembered in a way I would have liked." In the same interview Harry said that he wanted to remind people of the good work she had done, declaring firmly, "She had more guts than anyone else." Harry, like his mother, clearly wears his heart on his sleeve. In the words of one of his father's staff, "A lot of people look at Prince William and compare him in looks to his mother but, in reality, it is Harry who is more like his mother in many ways." Harry, like William before him, was granted his own coat of arms to mark his eighteenth birthday and, like William, he asked the Queen to authorize the inclusion of the red escallops from the Spencer family crest.

Below: Harry is not as academically successful as William but he has begun to outshine him at polo. The princes spend many weekends during the summer playing mainly at the Beaufort Polo Club or at Cirencester. Both grounds are near to Highgrove.

Above: More royal cost cutting? The princes take part in a charity "polo" match at Tidworth Polo Ground, Wiltshire, in July 2002.

Overleaf: The mainly affluent polo fraternity unsurprisingly attracts its fair share of supporters. The regular presence of two of Britain's most eligible bachelors has done wonders for audience figures, especially female.

Diana made sure that both her sons were aware of life outside the privileged confines of royal palaces. Just as she had taken William to see the homeless and AIDS victims, she took Harry to see seriously ill children at London's Brompton Hospital and to a refuge for the homeless called The Passage. Harry revealed that both of them were inspired by "the way she got close to people and went for the sort of charities and organizations that everybody else was scared to go near, such as landmines in the Third World, and things that nobody had done before – AIDS for example."

Diana had only just started this phase of her son's wider education when she died, and Harry admitted that when he was fifteen or sixteen the idea of following in his mother's footsteps began to grow in his mind. "I always wanted to do it, but especially after my mother died", he revealed in September 2002, and he added, "I would like to carry on the things that she didn't quite finish. I have always wanted to, but was too young." One of his aides added, "He wants to do something that is tough, cutting-edge

and challenging." Prince William's role, like his father's, is well defined, but Harry will have to carve out his own niche to find a role that is fulfiling to the monarchy, to society and to himself.

To mark his eighteenth birthday he carried out his first solo royal engagements, including a visit to sick children at London's Great Ormond Street Hospital. A family friend said, "William and Harry have a natural ability to be relaxed with children. They get it from their mother." Nevertheless, although clearly at ease, Harry found it daunting not to have his brother around as usual during a royal engagement. "It was very different. I've always had my father and brother there. At things like the Golden Jubilee, when we met crowds in The Mall, I just followed what they did and shook hands as they did. But it's definitely harder doing it on your own."

There was speculation that the party-loving Harry would celebrate the rest of his eighteenth birthday with a huge gathering of friends, possibly at Windsor Castle where his cousin Zara had held a riotous party earlier in the year. Instead he opted for a quiet celebration, just as William had in June 2000 when he missed the party thrown by the Queen on his eighteenth birthday in order to revise for his A levels. Asked what he had planned for his birthday, Harry replied, "Nothing. I'm not having a party or anything. My father offered me a birthday party at home but I turned it down. I don't actually like being the centre of attention." Then, in a touching tribute to Charles and William, he added that his birthday was going to be "a quiet day at home with my father and brother – my family". The close-knit bond between the three men once again has links with the past. During the war years the main core of the royal family was simply Charles's grandparents George VI and Queen Elizabeth and the two princesses. Following Princess Elizabeth's wedding in November 1947, her father wrote to remind her, "Our family, us four, the 'Royal Family' must remain together ...".

William and Harry frequently meet up at Highgrove. Harry spends most weekends there when he's free and William often flies down from St Andrews. Harry jokingly points out, "We've got a lot of computer games at Highgrove and, well, you can't play them on your own can you?" The two are now on more of an equal footing and work as a team. A few years ago the two-year age gap was more significant and Harry always had to fit in as the younger brother. On one occasion at Highgrove he was seen running down the stairs trying to do up his trousers at the same time. When asked why he was in such a rush, Harry snapped, "William's waiting for me, and if I'm late I'll get it in the neck."

While at Highgrove the princes follow the local hunts, particularly the Beaufort. They also play polo together and occasionally with their father at the Cirencester ground or the Beaufort Club. They have even formed their own Highgrove team with another experienced player. Harry has only been playing since he was sixteen but he has already left William far behind and hopes to spend at least some of his gap year improving his polo technique. Harry is regarded by professionals as a more aggressive player than his brother. John Lloyd, author of the *Pimm's Book of Polo,* agrees. "Harry is more of a daredevil. He's gutsier and really throws himself into the game. William is quite a shy boy by nature and gets nervous playing."

The princes enjoy the social aspect of the game as well. They mix with a tight-knit group of local friends, some of whom study at nearby Cirencester Agricultural College. William, as always, is discreet, particularly when he senses that the cameras are present. In the summer of 2001 photographs were taken of him chatting to farmer's daughter Emma Lippiatt at the Beaufort Club. Two weeks earlier Harry had been snapped playfully pouncing on her and throwing her over his shoulder, while his friends stood by laughing. Even enjoying innocent fun, the brothers clearly display their own style, with William always the more reticent and always mindful of his position.

Harry is the more daring and adventurous of the two brothers, and has tried his hand at paragliding and water skiing as well as riding motorbikes. The two enjoy skiing and have been to the slopes regularly since the early 1990s when Diana would take them to Lech in Austria early each spring and Charles would take them to Klosters, usually at Easter. Harry, according to one of his friends, "skis like he rides – very daringly and very competitively", while William is more cautious. Their ski guide Bruno Sprecher, admits that Harry is a pretty reckless downhill skier. "I have to hang on to him on black runs; the way he goes hell-bent I'm always afraid he'll have an accident."

Both brothers enjoy the traditional Windsor sports of shooting and stalking. They always stay at Sandringham for a few days after Christmas to attend the shoots organized by Prince Philip. Again there is a social aspect to these sports, as they are usually accompanied by their father, Princes Andrew and Edward and Peter Phillips. The same group meet up on the Balmoral estate during the late summer to go stalking. Since the Queen Mother's death, Charles has taken over her Birkhall estate, while the young princes stay a mile away at the cottage that the Queen has given them to use in the hope that they, like generations of the royal family before them, will come to love the privacy and isolation of the Deeside landscape.

Although the brothers enjoy their time together they are obviously beginning to move in separate social groups now that William is at university. The gradual move to more independent lifestyles began during William's

Left: An intrigued Harry scans the skyline for the approach of the Golden Jubilee flypast; historic and modern aircraft salute the Queen by flying down the Mall and over Buckingham Palace, 4 June 2002.

Right: Golden Jubilee weekend, and after a thanksgiving service at St Mary's Church in Swansea, the princes meet well-wishers in the city centre. During the service the bishop of Swansea announced for the benefit "of certain people who had a particular interest in the fortunes of England" that the latter had beaten Sweden 1–0 in the opening match of the World Cup.

gap year. Although the older prince clearly benefited from his time away, Harry's social life began a downward spiral that eventually ran temporarily out of control in the full glare of the media. A concerned William once again took on the role of Harry's adviser and protector.

The story of Harry's problems broke unexpectedly at the beginning of 2002. It was the dawn of the Queen's Golden Jubilee year, and she was at Sandringham with the Duke of Edinburgh and the ailing Queen Mother, while her offices in London were already outlining some of the plans for the summer's celebrations. But on 13 January, two Sunday newspapers revealed that Harry had been involved in a spate of drinking and cannabis-smoking the previous summer while he was still only sixteen. At the time Charles was away and William was on his gap year tour so neither could have stepped in to halt proceedings. Both of them must have known it was likely to happen since Harry had been spotted drinking and smoking when the family and their friends had shared a Mediterranean holiday on the Latsis yacht *Alexander* a few summers earlier.

The good thing about the story only breaking six months after the incidents happened was that Charles's staff at St James's Palace, after confirming that the stories were true, were straight away able to tell the media how Charles had taken immediate action. The prince, having

discussed the matter with William, sent his younger son for a day to Featherstone Lodge, a drug rehabilitation centre in south-east London, where he was shown the realities of the danger of the drugs culture.

Although Charles, like his sister and two brothers, is a very moderate drinker, he and his family must all have recalled his own brush with under-age drinking almost forty years earlier – the infamous "cherry brandy scandal". Charles was also sixteen at the time and on a private tour with a group of schoolfriends. They reached Stornaway Harbour on the Isle of Lewis where they were pursued by a group of tourists and onlookers, forcing the boys to duck into the Crown Hotel. Charles later recalled thinking, "My God! What do I do? I looked round and everybody was looking at

Above: Acknowledging the cheers of the crowd, William and Harry arrive for the "Party at the Palace", the pop concert held in the grounds of Buckingham Palace as part of the Queen's Golden Jubilee celebrations, the evening of 3 June 2002.

me. And I thought, 'I must have a drink ...' I thought you had to have alcohol in a bar, so I said 'Cherry Brandy'." At that moment a journalist walked in and the incident became world news.

When the news of Harry's escapade broke, he left Eton immediately to spend the day with William and Charles at Highgrove. William also invited Guy Pelly, one of the group that had been with Harry during the drinking sessions the previous summer. According to one of William's circle, "He admires the fact that Guy hasn't said anything himself about the affair." The following month the princes invited Pelly to join them to watch England's rugby team play Ireland at Twickenham.

The newspapers gleefully covered another fall from grace in the summer of 2002 when Harry was photographed drinking heavily at a party at the Beaufort Club. Of more concern to Charles were the photos taken of Harry smoking at the same polo club in August. Charles is a strong opponent of cigarettes and blames them for contributing to the deaths of his grandfather King George VI and aunt Princess Margaret, both of who were heavy smokers. Asked in September 2002 how he felt looking back over a year that had seen his drink and drugs difficulties paraded for all the world to see, Harry said simply, "That was a mistake, and I learned my lesson. It was never my intention to be that way."

It must be galling for Harry that while his private life makes critical headlines and he is characterized as the rebellious brother, William – who has smoked occasionally himself – is usually portrayed as diligent, conscientious and responsible. This is largely to do with the media's attitude. Thirty years earlier Princess Margaret complained about a similar imbalance in reports of her lifestyle. "When my sister and I were growing up, she was made out to be the goody goody one. That was boring, so the press tried to make out I was as wicked as hell."

For the boys who were brought solidly together through tragedy, the road to manhood hasn't been that easy. For Harry it must be reassuring to know that he can rely on a brother who is calm, well adjusted and mature beyond his years. For William it is even more reassuring to know that whatever lies in the future, he has the support of a brother who knows what it is like to live under the constant scrutiny of press and public alike.

CHAPTER FOUR

WILLIAM AND THE ROYAL FAMILY

illiam's great-grandfather, George VI, used to refer to the monarchy as "The Firm", and for the royal family living at Buckingham Palace was "living over the shop". For the past half century the firm has been in the capable hands of Elizabeth II. Her aim in the last years of her tenure is to ensure that nothing, but nothing, damages the smooth transition of power from her to Charles III and then on to the hope of the future, William V. The first meeting between the Queen and the future king occurred the morning after his birth. Staring down at the tiny bundle who would one day become the forty-second monarch since the Norman Conquest in 1066, she commented, "Thank goodness he hasn't got ears like his father."

During William's early years royal protocol was pretty far down on his list of priorities. William's behavioural low point was witnessed by over half a billion people worldwide when, at the age of four, he was a pageboy at the wedding of Sarah Ferguson and Prince Andrew. William, perched on a footstool far beyond his parents' reach, fidgeted through most of the service and stuck his tongue out at the bridesmaids.

A former courtier told the writer Graham Turner of the occasion when he was visiting and said to the young William and Harry, "The Queen will be here at tea-time." A baffled Harry said, "Who's the Queen?" The courtier described himself as "gobsmacked", adding, "I don't think William knew that she was called the Queen either. To them she was just 'Granny'."

Right: Four generations of the royal family leave St Paul's Cathedral after the thanksgiving service to mark the Queen Mother's hundredth birthday. Should the Queen follow her mother's example, she will have reigned for seventy-four years by the time of her centenary celebrations. Prince Charles will be in his seventy-eighth year and William will be forty-four.

Left: Baby William, safe in the arms of his nanny Barbara Barnes, has yet to learn that life as second in line to the throne would mean a lifetime of police security.

She may have been just "Granny" but William was eventually taught that every time he met her he had to bow to her, which must have seemed a bit odd, even to a youngster. To members of the royal family obeisance to the sovereign is second nature. In 2002, as the Queen left church after the 9 a.m. communion on Christmas morning, she opted to drive back to Sandringham while all the other royals walked. As her Jaguar shot past them, Philip, Charles, William and the other men bowed while Anne and the ladies curtsied. By now respect for the Queen is second nature for William. In July 1999, at the Cartier polo match at the Guards Club in Windsor, he joined Victoria Aitken, Katharine Bearman and Tamara Vestey for lunch. However, once the Queen arrived he put on his jacket, straightened his tie and made for the royal box where he greeted his royal granny with bow and a kiss on either cheek.

As time goes on the relationship between William and the Queen has deepened. Despite his Spencer looks, William has many strong Windsor characteristics, and is probably closer in personality to his grandmother than to any of his other relations. For her part the Queen has a great deal of affection for William and his brother, which Princess Diana confirmed when, shortly before her death, she told the BBC's Jennie Bond, "She adores William and Harry."

Elizabeth as a girl was reserved but very determined. She fell in love with Philip when she was only nineteen and became unofficially engaged the following year.

Above: 23 July 1986. The Westminster Abbey wedding of William's uncle Andrew, Duke of York to Sarah Ferguson. A bored and fractious four-year-old William wonders just how much longer the service is going to last.

Left: Royal children are favourite wedding attendants and William was no exception. The Princess Royal once complained of having to organize "yards of uncontrollable children."

While courtiers voiced their concerns, Queen Mary told a friend, "She will always know her own mind. There's something very steadfast and determined in her." William also has a strong, independent spirit. When a thanksgiving service was held at St Paul's to honour the victims of 11 September 2001, William wasn't included on the guest list and apparently made it known that he was irritated not to be invited.

Both the Queen and William are conscientious in their work routines. She is known to spend two or three hours a day working through the red boxes that are sent to her from Number 10 Downing Street, the Cabinet Office, the Home Office and the Foreign Office. She once told her assistant private secretary, "I'm quite an executive person", and her staff agree unequivocally. "She never hangs on to papers", says one aide. "They invariably come back dealt with and, where necessary, annotated with instructions as to what we're to do."

William applies himself to his academic life with the same determination. Because his eighteenth birthday fell in the middle of his A level exams

Below: Trooping the Colour in 1985 and William, alongside his childhood playmates Lord Frederick Windsor and Peter Phillips, watches an RAF flypast from the balcony of Buckingham Palace, while Diana keeps a friendly eye on them.

he declined any form of celebration until they were over. When the Queen gave a massive joint birthday party at Windsor castle to celebrate the one hundredth, seventieth, fiftieth and fortieth birthdays of, respectively, the Queen Mother, Princess Margaret, the Princess Royal and the Duke of York, William missed it in order to concentrate on revising, even though he was less than a mile away at Eton.

Despite half a century in the most public of roles, the Queen is still surprisingly shy. A former lady-in-waiting recalled the teenage Elizabeth attending a Guards cocktail party. "She was so paralysed that she could hardly speak." Fifty years later she is often quite reserved. A former private secretary says, "It is very odd to watch her sidle into a room, she doesn't even try to make an appearance." William would sympathize with that, since he also hates the spotlight. As a teenager he blushed easily and stared at the world from under a blond shield of hair that he grew long deliberately so that he could hide behind it. Leaving a Guards Club polo match

Above: 17 June 1989. Another Trooping the Colour, and this time Harry was old enough to join William and Diana in the Queen Mother's carriage procession. The boys wave as aircraft of the Royal Air Force fly over Buckingham Palace. Behind them their mother, grandparents and great aunt, Princess Margaret, look equally delighted.

with his father in 1996, the fourteen-year-old William held one hand across his face as photographers snapped at the car. Two years later, as he joined the royal family for the Queen Mother's birthday lunch party at Clarence House, he shrank back during the group appearance when crowds chanted, "We want William!"

Both the Queen and William are modest in their approach to life. Lunch guests at the log cabins she uses on the Balmoral estate still find it unnerving to watch the Queen lay the table, pass round the food, lean over to collect the plates away afterwards and then brush the floors. William has an equally hands-on approach, as became obvious during his time in Chile as a Raleigh International volunteer. He was filmed yawning at 6.15 a.m. as he stoked the fire and made the porridge. The most striking image of his ten-week stay was that of the future king snapping on his rubber gloves and cleaning the communal lavatories. Elizabeth II may never have gone that far, but one house guest recalled "seeing her going round the house at Sandringham with a soda siphon and blotting paper mopping up after one of Prince Charles's incontinent puppies".

Both grandmother and grandson use humour as a safety valve to survive the often dull routine of royal life. The Queen, ever conscious of the dignity of her role in public, has deadpan humour down to a fine art. Once, on a visit to the Milk Marketing Board, she came face to face with an intricate plastic display on the wall. "And what's that?" she asked.

Below: The Queen and Prince William have many similarities. Both are naturally shy and have a modest but light-hearted approach to life; both are happy in their own company.

"It's a cow's vagina, Your Majesty", explained her host. "Oh ask a silly question ..." she replied. William's sense of humour is more slapstick. During the ITV television programme to celebrate his eighteenth birthday, he was filmed making paella with a fellow student at Eton. When his friend dropped a huge piece of chicken into a frying pan full of rice and vegetables and half the pan's contents slopped over the sides on to the cooker, William fell about laughing, hand clasped over his mouth in a gesture that was pure Diana.

The Queen is a gifted mimic and has been known to imitate anyone from pompous mayors to Margaret Thatcher. Her impression of the Ulster politician, the Reverend Ian Paisley, is legendary in royal circles. William might not be hot on taking off members of parliament, but in Chile the cameras caught him doing a pretty mean Ali G – the comic character created by Sacha Baron Cohen – as he took over the role of the DJ for the evening, dedicating tunes "to all those of you out there looking for lurrrve".

Edward VIII may have put his emotional life before his duty to Britain and its empire, but his niece is made of sterner stuff. In her fifty-plus years on the throne she has always been conscientious, hardworking and dutiful. To her generation – the Second World War generation – personal sacrifice was a guiding principle, and she's aware that for William effectively to sacrifice his personal life for the sake of the monarchy is a

Left: Don't tell granny! William, Harry and their cousins hitch a ride in Queen Victoria's ivory phaeton which the Queen uses when she reviews her army regiments at Trooping the Colour on Horse Guards Parade. The carriage was waiting to be returned to the Royal Mews when it became too much of a temptation.

Right: Four of the Queen's grandchildren enjoy a day on the ski slopes. William leads Harry, and their cousins Beatrice and Eugenie of York as they prepare to pose for photographers on the first day of their break. The children were in Klosters for a holiday with their mothers.

challenge that won't be easy. In 1992, she voiced her concerns about the future in the television documentary *Elizabeth R*. "If you live in this sort of life", she began, "you live very much by tradition and continuity ... As far as I'm concerned you know what you're going to be doing two months ahead, even next year. I think that this is what the younger members (of the royal family) find difficult – the regimented side of it."

In the same documentary she confided that what has helped her over the years was her early preparation. "I have a feeling", she said, "that in the end, probably, training is the answer to a great many things. You can do lots if you're properly trained and I hope I have been." She hasn't directly trained William of course, but she has always been there to offer advice – we know that in his Eton days he occasionally walked to nearby Windsor Castle for tea with granny and a chat about life at the college. Behind the scenes, as head of the monarchy, she has taken a keen interest in the education of a future king. As the royal expert Brian Hoey pointed out in a recent biography of the Queen, "William's education and training for his eventual role is supervised personally by the Queen, with constant advice from the Duke of Edinburgh." Prince Charles knows that anything that has implications for his sons' role in the Royal Family must be brought to the attention of his mother. "When it comes to the future of his sons, he knows he dare not go against the wishes of the Queen", says Hoey.

Right: By the time of the Queen Mother's ninety-fourth birthday in August 1994, William, now twelve, was already as tall as his great grandmother. Eighty-two years separated them but they clearly relished their precious time together.

Left: Following her death in March 2002, William revealed that one of his favourite memories of his great grandmother was helping her up the steps of the Deanery at Windsor after attending an Easter day service at St George's Chapel. The Queen Mother joked, "Keep doing that for people and you will go a long way."

Although she believes that you should put duty before personal pleasure the Queen more than anyone is sympathetic to William's need to have fun while he is still young and free from the ties of marriage and royal duties. Losing his mother in the middle of his teenage years was traumatic enough without having to begin royal duties just a few years later. The Queen can't imagine what William must have gone through when Diana died, but she can certainly understand to a degree since her beloved father died when she was only twenty-five. She not only lost a father but she also lost a complete way of life, as Princess Diana admitted to Jennie Bond, "She became Queen at such a tender age, she must have been like a startled rabbit wondering how to contend with this role."

After only four years of marriage she was obliged to sacrifice her private life forever. In nearly eight decades the Queen has only once "opted out" when, in 1949, she flew to the island of Malta for several months to stay with Prince Philip when he was stationed on the island with the navy. For the only time in her life the young Elizabeth experienced what it must be like to be "ordinary" and away from the pressures of royal life and media. Her biographer Douglas Keay paints a vivid picture of this period, "There were parties, picnics, shops to wander in and out of, carry-

Left: An unmistakeable warmth as Zara Phillips jokes with William as they pose for the cameras with four generations of the royal family before a lunch party to celebrate the Queen Mother's ninety-eighth birthday at Clarence House, her London home.

Below: A fun moment as William accepts a posy from an admirer as he arrives with Sophie Rhys-Jones for a lunch to celebrate the Queen's Golden Wedding in November 1997.

ing her cane basket over her arm. In her Jacqmar headscarf, dirndl skirt and sunglasses it was easy for others not to recognize the future Queen."

It is because this most private of women has rarely experienced absolute privacy that she has backed completely William's desire to remain a private citizen for as long as possible. As one senior Buckingham Palace insider put it, "The Queen and Prince William have a very close relationship and she is able to share with him many experiences of what it is like to reconcile the role of monarch with that of leading a happy and balanced life."

In her 1998 Christmas broadcast the Queen admitted from experience that the members of the younger generation do not want a constant lecture from older relatives. "It is not always easy", she said, "for those in their teens and twenties to believe that someone of my age, of the older generation, might have something useful to say to them", but she acknowledged that learning is a two-way process and that she is constantly being taught surprising lessons by her

Right: 4 June 2002. Fun for Harry, William and Peter Phillips as they watch the Queen's Golden Jubilee pageant from their seats on the Queen Victoria Memorial in front of Buckingham Palace.

grandchildren. "My own grandchildren ... have a remarkable grasp of modern technology", she admitted in the broadcast. "They are lucky to have the freedom to travel and learn about foreign cultures at an age when the appetite for learning is keen." One courtier confirmed, "William is able to tell the Queen about his generation, and what he and Harry are up to. They talk about many of the things that every grandson and grandmother talk about, especially their shared love of riding." Another member of staff agrees. "He has clear and constructive views and the Queen finds some of his ideas intriguing."

William enjoyed a close relationship with the Queen Mother. Although born during the second Boer War (1899–1902), the Queen Mother was rarely absorbed by the past, but always concentrated on the future. This was the lady who asked her equerry, William de Rouet, "Do men go out with girls or 'birds' these days?" When he replied, "If you're 'with it' you go out with birds", she retorted, "But I *am* 'with it', William."

The Queen Mother loved stories about William's time at Eton. She particularly delighted in stories about him getting into trouble. "She had a young sense of humour", recalled William. "Every single thing that went wrong or was funny for any reason she laughed herself stupid about – it

kept us all sane." William was constantly amazed by her energy and vitality at such a great age. "I looked up to her because what an achievement it was to live to 101. It was a pleasure to sit next to her at lunch. She always had such great war stories, and to hear them from her, it really brought it all to life. She was incredible."

On the day that he started at St Andrews University he called in to see his great grandmother at Birkhall, near Balmoral. After "an amazing lunch" the prince prepared to set off for university full of anxieties. Typically the Queen Mother found the right words to lift his nervousness and tension. "As she said goodbye, she said 'Any good parties, invite me down.' I said, 'Yes,' but there was no way. I knew full well that if I invited her down she would dance me under the table." As he grew up, William became more protective of her. He said, "My favourite photograph of us together was a picture of me aged about nine or ten helping the Queen Mother up the steps of Windsor Castle. I remember the

Above: April 15 1999 and William carried out his first major solo engagement when he became a godfather to Prince Konstantine Alexios, the five-month-old grandson of ex-King Constantine of Greece. The ceremony was held in the Greek church in London's Bayswater. Besides carrying the baby, William had to carry his left arm in a sling following a recent operation on a broken finger.

moment because she said to me, 'Keep doing that for people and you will go a long way in life'."

The member of the royal family who perhaps more than any other realizes the pain that William must have gone through because of the breakdown of his parents' marriage and the tragedy in Paris is his grandfather, the Duke of Edinburgh. Prince Philip's childhood was insecure to say the least. His family was exiled from Greece, the country of his birth. His mother was diagnosed with paranoid schizophrenia and for eight years was confined to sanatoria in Germany and Switzerland. Between the ages of eight and fifteen Philip did not see his mother or receive so much as a birthday card from her.

Philip's father also deserted him. Prince Andrew of Greece established a playboy existence near the casinos of Monte Carlo with his mistress the Comtesse de La Bigne, and died in near-poverty in 1944 when Philip was twenty-three. Philip went to Monte Carlo to collect his father's few belongings. Poignantly the Comtesse gave him Andrew's signet ring and he has worn it ever since. Probably the most distressing experience in Philip's youth was the death of his favourite sister Cecile who was killed in a air crash with her husband and two children in 1937 when Philip was sixteen. According to a friend he "never forgot the profound shock" with which he heard the news, and for many months carried in his pocket a small piece of the tangled metal of the aircraft.

Philip is often portrayed as a remote authoritarian figure, largely because of his somewhat strained relationship with Prince Charles. Surprisingly, he is actually fond of children and has developed a strong relationship with all his grandchildren, particularly Peter Phillips and Prince William. Philip's cousin, Countess Mountbatten of Burma, told one biographer recently, "He loves small children and he's very good with them – even sweet – I've seen him with ours when they were younger and he couldn't be more patient or understanding."

William has reciprocated this affection over the years, asking for instance if Philip would walk next to him in Diana's funeral procession (as the procession disappeared momentarily when it passed under the archway of the old Admiralty building Philip could be seen briefly touching William in the small of his back in a gesture of support). More than a year later in January 1999 William decided against joining Charles and Harry on a skiing break at Klosters and stayed at Sandringham to go shooting with Philip.

One of the dilemmas of life in the royal family is discovering whom exactly you can and cannot trust. As William knows from experience, detectives, housekeepers, valets and even private secretaries are keen to cash in on even the briefest of royal associations. Royal children soon realize that the most loyal friends are in fact their own relations. The Queen's closest friends were probably her mother and sister. William's closest friends, besides Prince Harry, are probably his cousins Peter and Zara.

Princess Anne's two children played regularly with William and Harry during the royal reunions for Christmas at Sandringham and for Easter at Windsor. Peter and Zara grew up at Gatcombe, the Princess Royal's home near Highgrove. As children they would come over to play on Broadfield Farm which was run by David Wilson on behalf of the Duchy of Cornwall. William and Zara could often be seen dodging around the massive high-tech grain store that dominates the landscape. As one member of the Highgrove staff put it at the time, "When William and Zara get together they are a precocious pair of rascals."

These days the two still meet whenever possible at the respective estates when they either enjoy outdoor pursuits or simply laze around chatting and listening to music. As children Peter and Zara would pass on to William and Harry the ponies that they had learned to ride on. In later life this arrangement was reversed and William asked Zara to look after his polo ponies during his gap year.

The Queen regards Peter and Zara as good influences on William, especially after it became apparent that many people in his social circle had admitted to taking cocaine. The two cousins also appreciate just how difficult it is to survive the break-up of a royal marriage under the unrelenting scrutiny of the media. Their parents, Princess

Below: The Duke of Edinburgh doesn't suffer fools gladly, but clearly has a great deal of time for his grandson. Philip gives William a proud smile as they leave St Paul's Cathedral, London in June 2000.

Above: Elizabeth II celebrating fifty years as Queen and looking radiant at the end of her Jubilee celebrations as she shares a moment with the man who will one day be king.

Anne and Captain Mark Phillips, announced their official separation in August 1989 when Peter was twelve and Zara eight.

The tragedy of Diana's death brought the cousins closer still. Peter and Zara went immediately to Balmoral where they spent the week walking, talking, playing CDs and just simply being there for William and Harry. Peter and Zara often tease William, who is naturally more introverted and shy than they are. When crowds cheered for William at the royal photo-call for the Queen Mother's birthday, it was Zara who nudged him and poked fun, helping to put all the adulation into perspective.

According to a member of the royal household Peter is, "uncomplicated, charming and not in the least pernickety and has had the most normal upbringing of all the royal children". He is the Queen's eldest grandson and arguably Prince Philip's favourite since he enjoys shooting and is a fan of so many sports from rugby to Formula One racing. At the same time, he is in a sense an ordinary citizen since Anne refused the Queen's offer of a title when she married in 1973. Barring any official honour by the Queen, he will always be known as Mr Peter Phillips. Anne and Mark sent him to the local school in Minchinhampton near Gatcombe and he managed a three-year degree at Exeter University without any hassle from the media.

William envies Peter's relative freedom and has always looked up to him, and at times even hero-worshipped him. It was widely reported that he was even emulating Peter's style at the Cartier polo tournament in July 1999. According to one newspaper the seventeen-year-old prince "seemed the image of Princess Anne's twenty-year-old son right down to the trademark wraparound sunglasses. And, when he left, minus the shades and tie, the stunning similarity became even more apparent."

Zara has an even greater zest for life than either Peter or William. In 1998 she had her tongue pierced in a tattoo parlour in Elgin, Scotland, and more recently she had her navel pierced. In her gap year she had a romance with a teenage barman in Australia, and while in New Zealand managed a bungee jump into a 40-metre (132-foot) gorge above the Kawarau River. In December 2000 she overturned her Land Rover into a ditch during an early morning drive from Gatcombe to nearby stables, and the following year she was spotted having a brawl with her then boyfriend Richard Johnson after a row in an Oxford pub. Despite her colourful lifestyle, Zara receives a largely sympathetic press, and the newspapers have applauded her skill as a horsewoman from three-day eventing to flat racing as well as her fashion sense and her down-to-earth approach to royal life. This after all is the woman who arrived at Royal Ascot and got changed in a pub-

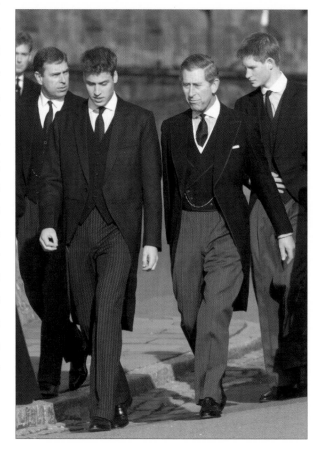

Below: A sad beginning to Jubilee year. The Duke of York, William, Charles and Harry walk from the private apartments at Windsor Castle to St George's Chapel for the funeral service for Princess Margaret who died on 9 February at the age of seventy-one.

Above: A monarch, two future monarchs, two dukes and a princess mourn the passing of the last Queen Empress of Britain.

Overleaf: 4 June 2002. Eight weeks after the Queen Mother's funeral, the Queen and Prince Philip watch the Golden Jubilee celebrations surrounded by their family.

lic loo in the car park. It would be virtually impossible for William to get away with the same lifestyle, but he has obviously learned a lot from her about how you can be a key player in the royal family and still lead a relatively normal life.

Unlike William and Harry, Peter and Zara know that they will never have to undertake public duties. Nevertheless they are fiercely loyal to the crown and behave with tact and decorum during family appearances for birthdays and anniversaries, and the formal occasions such as the Golden Jubilee. It must be reassuring for William to know that when he eventually succeeds to the throne he will always have his cousins around to offer advice and trustworthy support.

CHAPTER FIVE

WILLIAM THE STUDENT

Prince Philip once said, "You can't train a boy to be King. But if you train him to be a man then he can be anything." The future Charles III and many of his predecessors could tell Philip from bitter experience that this is easier said than done. The education of most of the British monarchs since Victoria seems to have been a combination of ill-trained tutors, overbearing royal parents and non-academic pupils. Victoria's heir, the future Edward VII, was made to study from 8 a.m. to 7 p.m. from Monday to Saturday. His father, Prince Albert, insisted on a daily report on his son's progress and instructed his tutor that the boy must be exhausted at the end of the day. The tutor found the prince "extremely disobedient, impertinent ... and unwilling to submit to discipline". Albert called Sir George Combe, the leading phrenologist of his day, who examined the young boy's cranium and diagnosed a "feeble" brain.

Perhaps as a result of this inhumane treatment, Edward decided to appoint the fair-minded Reverend John Dalton to teach his own son, the future George V. George, however, was a poor pupil and, according to Dalton, was "deficient in even the most elementary subjects". His spelling and grammar were insecure – throughout his life he would write the name of his country's greatest playwright as "Sheakspeare" – and his French and German were embar-

Right: A far cry from royal palaces. Carrying a hard hat and gloves the future king is set for a long day's work in the remote Chilean community of Tortel during his gap year travels before starting university.

Left: And so to school. 24 September 1985 and William greets the head teacher on his first day at Mrs Mynor's Nursery School, watched by Diana, who later confessed to breaking down on her return to Kensington Palace.

rassingly poor despite extensive time spent in both countries.

The next generation fared little better. George appointed Henry Hansell to tutor his sons, the future Edward VIII and the brother who would succeed him as George VI. Hansell was appointed not because of his intellectual ability but because he was a keen yachtsman and golfer. Deeply aware of his own inadequacies, the tutor suggested that the boys would be much better off if they were sent to a prep school but the idea was vetoed by their father.

Queen Elizabeth's mother, then Duchess of York, had hated her own brief visits to a London day school, and wanted her two daughters to be educated at home. In 1933 she appointed as tutor a twenty-three-year-old Scots girl called Marion Crawford. Miss Crawford had trained at Edinburgh's Moray House before taking up the post as tutor to the two children of the Duchess's sister Rose. In *The Little Princesses*, Crawford's account of life with the Yorks, the governess later recalled the

Left: January 1987 and a brave four-and-a-half-year- old prince waves to the photographers on his first day at Wetherby School, where he was to study for the next three years.

Left: The annual school nativity play can be embarrassing at the best of times, without having it documented by the cameras. Here an apprehensive prince passes the assembled media pack outside Wetherby School.

Right: The summer of 1989 and William competes in that stalwart tradition of school sports days, the egg and spoon race. Later he would cheer on Charles and Diana who always joined the mums' and dads' races.

Duchess's recipe for the future Queen's education. "To spend as long as possible in the open air, to enjoy to the full the pleasures of the country, to be able to dance and draw and appreciate music, to acquire good manners and perfect deportment, and to cultivate all the distinctly feminine graces." Later she would add Bible reading, poetry, history and geography to the list. To prepare her for her future role, Princess Elizabeth was also given twice-weekly lessons in constitutional history by Sir Henry Marten, the vice-provost of Eton.

In deciding the type of education that would be suitable for the future King William, Prince Charles would almost certainly have been aware of a century-and-a-half of mismanagement as well as his own, often tormented, education. Charles was initially educated by a Scots-born governess, Catherine Peebles, who had previously tutored the Queen's cousin, Princess Alexandra. At the age of eight he was sent to Hill House, a "pre-preparatory" school in west London where he shone at art and reading, but failed to grasp the basics of mathematics. From Hill House he went to Cheam School in Berkshire, another break with palace tradition.

Although the Queen Mother badly wanted her favourite grandchild to go to Eton, Charles was sent to Gordonstoun, his father's old school overlooking Scotland's north-east coast. Charles was desperately lonely and he failed to relate to the Spartan regime that had so inspired his father. Although he begged to leave after two terms, it was made clear to him that there was no alternative and he would have to cope with it.

Both Charles and Diana wanted William to start school at a young age. The couple settled on Mrs Mynor's Nursery School in Notting Hill Gate, less than a mile away from their Kensington Palace apartments. William started there in September 1985 at the age of three and was welcomed outside by head teacher Jane Mynors as well as 150 photographers who had been encamped there since dawn. William's education began in Cygnet Class where a report, now in the royal archives, reveals that he was very keen on reading and loved to write his name. He was part of a class of twelve pupils and one detective. By the time he was promoted to the Big Swan Class, William had acted in two plays, watched by his proud parents and Prince Harry, and had also sung solo. The palace records tell us, "Prince William was very popular with the other children, and was known for his kindness, sense of fun, and quality of thoughtfulness."

After fifteen months William moved on to nearby Wetherby School, where he was to stay for the next three years. It was noted here that he had a flair for English and spelling. He had also clearly inherited his mother's love of swimming, and by the time he was seven and in Form 4 he had won the Grunfield Cup for the best overall swimming style. While at Wetherby, William sang in three Christmas concerts as well as acting in the 1990 school play, *The Saga of Erik Nobeard or A Viking Nonetheless.*

William went on to spend five years at Ludgrove Preparatory School in Berkshire where he was studying when his parents announced their separation in December 1992. During his time at Ludgrove William developed into a good all-rounder. At the age of ten he won the junior essay prize. He was also the captain of the hockey and football teams and represented the school in

Below: William, wearing his brand new satchel, tries his best to look sophisticated as he starts another new term at Wetherby. Harry, on his first day, looks suitably awe-struck by his brother.

Right: September 1995 and the thirteen-year-old prince begins his five-year stay at Eton College. Charles and Diana put aside their private differences and present a united front as the family walk back to Manor House after a tour of the main buildings. Once again Harry is there to offer moral support.

cross-country running. To the delight of Prince Philip, when he was twelve William won the Cliddesden Salver for clay pigeon shooting. Diana was more impressed that William was developing a caring side to his nature. For two years running he took part in sponsored walks for the Wokingham and District Association for the Elderly.

Charles certainly felt he had William's best interests at heart when it came to choosing a senior school. Eton College has strong links with the British monarchy. It was founded by Henry VI (1421–71) in 1440 as the Royal College of Our Lady at Eton by Windsor. Henry VIII (1491–1547) seized many of the college's properties, including the site of St James's Palace. Better relations were fostered under Charles II (1630–85) who, according to the diarist Samuel Pepys (1633–1703), rated its beer very highly. George III (1738–1820) also had close links with Eton and, since the early nineteenth century, the college has marked his birthday, 4 June, with a day of celebration. The distinctive black frock coat worn by all the boys dates back to the mourning for this king. More recently the Queen's uncle Henry, Duke of Gloucester, was a student at the college and her cousins the present Dukes of Gloucester and Kent and Prince Michael of Kent also went to school there.

The Princess of Wales also had strong ties with Eton. Her father was a pupil during the early years of the Second World War. He wasn't at all gifted academically but was remembered by another peer, Lord Montagu of Beaulieu, as "always a very gentle sweet person. I never heard him raise his voice against anybody." Diana's brother Charles, the present Earl Spencer, was also a pupil at Eton during the later 1970s and the princess admired the way the college was run in a family atmosphere under the headmaster, the housemasters and their wives.

William's housemaster was an Ulsterman, Dr Andrew Gailey, who supervised Eton's Manor House with the help of his wife Shauna. Completing the family was Christopher Stuart-Clark, who was to be

Above: William signs the college register on his first day at Eton in one of the first photographs that show he is left-handed. Initially William wrote his name in the wrong column and a solicitous Diana shows him where he should write his name.

William's personal tutor, and Elizabeth Heathcote, the matron. In an interview to mark his eighteenth birthday and his final weeks at Eton William was asked what he would miss most when he left. Without hesitating he replied, "I'll miss my friends, and Dr Gailey, who has been a tremendous support to me."

Unlike the other boys who are always referred to by their surnames, the prince was called William by his teachers and William Wales on paper. His other main privilege was to be given an *en suite* room while the other forty-nine boys in Manor House shared bathrooms. William was joined at Manor House by three friends – Andrew Charlton, John Richards and Harry Walsh – who had all been at Ludgrove with the prince. He was also joined

Right: The following morning with his parents and brother. First day nerves safely out of the way, a more relaxed William leads a stream of classmates from Manor House for their first day of lessons. The Eton uniform of black tailcoat, waistcoat and pin-striped trousers were originally mourning clothes for King George III in 1820 and have remained unchanged.

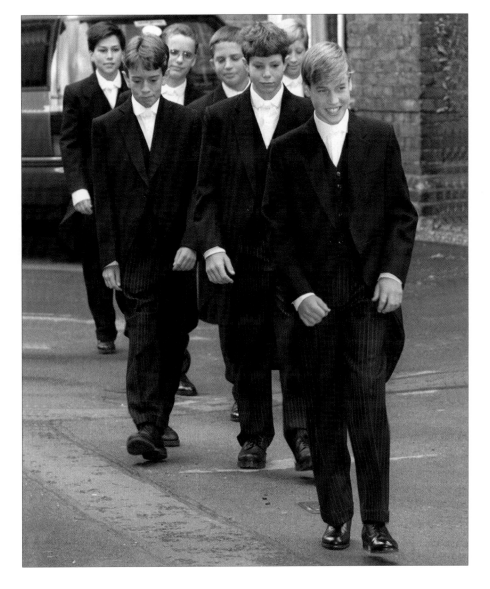

Left: Shielded from the public gaze, a pensive looking William alone with his thoughts as he prepares to face the end of his happy time at Eton College.

by another prince – Nirajan of Nepal – who was shot dead six years later by his elder brother Crown Prince Dipendra during a horrific massacre of eleven members of his family.

William proved to be far more academically gifted than any of his royal relatives. At the age of fifteen he passed GCSEs in science, Latin and French, to the delight of Diana who famously admitted to being as "thick as a plank". The following summer he managed to pass nine more GCSEs, gaining A grades in English, history and languages and B grades in all the others. The royal family was said to be "privately delighted" that William had been so successful despite the trauma of his mother's death.

In his last two years at Eton, William held positions of authority. At Gordonstoun, Charles had been a prefect, a house captain and eventually head boy. William, in turn, won the Sword of Honour as best cadet in the Eton College Combined Cadet Force, an honour that would have delighted Diana's father, whose favourite role at Eton had been as a company sergeant-major in the Eton College Officer Training Corps. William was also elected to be a member of Pop, Eton's elite group of nineteen elected prefects responsible for supervising the school's 1,260 boys. Among the privileges of being a Pop is an entitlement to wear colourful waistcoats instead of the traditional black ones, and William was happy to pose in his favourite Union Jack design for his official eighteenth birthday photos.

William's A level passes in the summer of 2000 confirmed his position as one of the brightest royals. Having obtained an A in geography, a B in History and a C in biology, he secured his place at St Andrews University on merit. In the previous generation, Charles had only managed to get a B in history and a C in French but still gained a place at Trinity College, Cambridge, while when Prince Edward arrived at the same university, having gained just a C in English and a D in history and politics, the undergraduates signed a petition against favouritism.

Prince Charles was also particularly keen for his son to have a break before starting university so that he could see something of the world before beginning to undertake public duties and while the British media was still respecting his privacy. At the age of seventeen Charles spent a year studying at Geelong Grammar School in Australia, much of it at the school's

Left: While many students used their own laptop computers in their rooms, surprisingly William was not one of them. Instead he opted to use one of four computers in a communal study room at Manor House.

Timbertop camp in the outback. Here the students fended for themselves, preparing their own food, cutting trees for heating and making long and arduous hikes in the outlying hills.

William enjoyed a similarly challenging role when he joined fifteen other volunteers for a ten-week Raleigh International project in the remote community of Tortel, deep in the heart of the Andes. Here William slept on the floor, cleaned the toilets, chopped firewood and made some "absolutely foul" porridge. Television coverage of the visit gave a glimpse of William's natural affinity with children when he acted as a classroom assistant in the nursery school. The six-year-olds took it in turn to leap on to the prince's back and forced him to walk around the room carrying them. He has clearly inherited his mother's affinity with children.

During his year off, William also joined his father's regiment, the Welsh Guards, to take part in a training exercise in the jungles of Belize. Then, in September 2000 he headed for Mauritius to carry out an educational project with the Royal Geographical Society. After the Chilean expedition that followed, William completed his gap year with a period working on an English farm and a four-month journey across Africa. The visit included tracking with the Masai tribes in the Serengeti as well as an educational

Above: During his final year at Eton, William was elected a member of Pop, the elite body of twenty-one prefects that was originally founded in 1811 and which is a self-electing group. Members have the right to supervise, discipline and, where necessary, to fine junior pupils.

trip to the Lewa Downs reserve in the beautiful foothills of Mount Kenya.

Ironically, given the vast amount of travel and the exotic locations, William's favourite part of his year off was the short time he spent much closer to home. "The best bit was in England", he told a journalist before starting university. "I loved working on a farm, before foot and mouth, which is partly why I've got so much sympathy for the farmers who have suffered so much from it. It was the best part of my year. I enjoyed the fact that I was brought in as a hand and was paid and was just another guy on the farm. I got my hands dirty, did all the chores and had to get up at 4 a.m. I got to see a completely different lifestyle." William's comments weren't just part of a well-choreographed PR exercise. Out of the fifty-one societies available for pupils at Eton, William chose to join just one, the Agricultural Society, in which he eventually served as secretary, clearly showing that he shares his family's concerns for the rural environment.

William was, however, diplomatic in revealing why he chose St Andrews University as opposed to Oxford or Cambridge, where three future kings – Edward VII, Edward VIII and Prince Charles – all studied. "I didn't

Right: William checking the progress of his chicken paella dinner. Cookery is one of the options in Eton's general studies programme, and an intriguing choice for the man who will one day host state banquets.

want to go to an English university", William commented shortly before his arrival at college, "because I've lived there and wanted to get away to try somewhere else. I also knew that I'd be seeing a lot of Wales in the future. And I do love Scotland ... and I thought St Andrews had a real community feeling."

The nineteen-year-old prince arrived at St Andrews in September 2001 to start a four-year history of art course. He was based initially at St Salvator's Hall, one of eleven halls of residence, where once again he was given a slightly larger suite of rooms to accommodate his ever-present security team. His much-publicized arrival brought with it the "Wills factor", which altered the normal male/female ratio, thanks to a forty-four per cent increase in applications to the university, mainly from girls.

Life in a small university town can be tough, even if you're not a prince. When Charles was at Cambridge in the late 1960s he wrote, "I feel as though I am in a zoo. There are people wandering about everywhere staring at everything that moves and if it happens to be me they stare and point even more." One of the reasons that prompted William's choice of St

Above: During his time in Patagonia, William proved that he has inherited his mother's affinity with children. During a visit to a local nursery school, six-year-old Alejandro Heredia jumped on to William's back and ordered him to gallop round the room.

Left: Wearing his Raleigh International sweatshirt, William snatches a few moments' peace to read a book. Bed was a space on the floor among fifteen other volunteers in a cold and damp disused nursery classroom.

Right: One of the group's tasks was the building of a wooden walkway, a vital link between houses. William helped to haul the huge supports into place before knocking them into the ground with a sledgehammer.

Below: The volunteers took turns to wake up at 6 a.m. to prepare breakfast for the others. William made porridge that he admitted was "absolutely foul", and promised to make some for his father on his return to Britain.

Andrews was its remoteness and relative inaccessibility for the London paparazzi and the busloads of tourists. William was even able to take part in the university's traditional Raisin Monday in the November of his first term at St Andrew's. Around a thousand students wearing fancy dress have a shaving-foam fight in the quad as part of an annual event that dates back to the fifteenth century; William painted his head blue and covered himself in foam as part of the prank.

By the time he had started his second term it was rumoured that William was unhappy and had not settled in at the university. One report claimed that he had spent only four out of seventeen weekends at St Andrews, despite having stated on his arrival, "I want to go to university and have fun. I want to go there and be an ordinary student. I'm not a party animal, but I like to go out like anyone else." In fact he chose to spend his weekends at Highgrove with Charles and Harry, dining with friends in Edinburgh or else staying at the private home on the Queen's Balmoral estate that had been given to him. It was

Previous pages: The Operation Raleigh expedition was a life-changing experience for someone whose every move at home is watched and scrutinized by people. "I wanted to get out and see a bit of the world at the same time as helping people", he recalled later. For a few short weeks he was able to do both.

Left: September 2001 and the latest phase in a long academic career. Nineteen-year-old William arrives at St Andrews University on the first day of a four-year history of art course. With hands thrust deeply into his pockets and a sidelong glance at the press, William clearly wishes he could arrive as unobtrusively as all the other students.

even reported that he was considering either changing courses or even university, as he was bored and lonely at St Andrews.

Life improved and became more companionable for William at the start of the second year when he decided to move out of the university halls of residence and rented a Georgian apartment in the town. One of his new flatmates was Fergus Boyd, who had lived in the same corridor as William at St Salvators. Besides the detective, the other new flatmate was Kate Middleton, who is also studying history of art. Their friendship was noticed by the media in April 2002 when William was photographed at a charity fashion show in which Kate went down the catwalk wearing a see-through black lace dress.

The St Andrews system works on a module and credit basis, which means students have to study more than one subject until third year honours. In his second year at the university William opted to make up his credits with first year moral philosophy, which has added three lectures and a tutorial to his weekly workload.

William again proved that he is a keen sports player. There are no classes at the university on Wednesday afternoons and the prince takes advantage of the free time to train for rugby and Sunday league football, which he plays for St Salvators. He is also an avid member of the university's water polo team.

William was much happier in his second year at the university and spent more weekends at St Andrews than he did in the first year. He has frequently been spotted in the Ma Bells pub in the basement of the Golf Hotel and also visits the Byre Theatre in Abbey Street on the other side of town. Having emerged from the secure confines of prep school and Eton, William has had the opportunity to lead a relatively independent life during his year off and during his time at St Andrews. In a life that will always be under media scrutiny this might be the last phase of privacy in an increasingly public life.

CHAPTER SIX

WILLIAM AND FASHION

William is attractive, presentable, second in line to the British throne and the son of a major fashion icon, so it was inevitable that he would come under the scrutiny of fashion writers, designers and market researchers. Just as happened to his famously elegant mother, William's every new accessory from his emblazoned sweaters to his wraparound shades is analyzed, admired and apparently copied by his contemporaries. Before he reached the age of sixteen the prince had already been voted "the world's most fanciable male", "one of the top 100 beautiful people" and "one of the planet's best dressers".

The House of Windsor has always had an ambivalent attitude to fashion. The Queen, like her mother, has tended to remain faithful to a formula of classic designs teamed with matching hats, handbags, shoes and pearls. According to her governess Marion Crawford, Princess Elizabeth "never cared a fig" how she was dressed. Despite having to appear in bejewelled magnificence for state dinners, openings and visits, Elizabeth II has always shirked the ostentatious power dressing that so enthralled her namesake, Elizabeth I. One of her earliest couturiers, Norman Hartnell, recalled, "One did not feel that she was really interested in clothes", and over the years she has been labelled "frumpy", "dowdy" and "matronly".

Right: No mistaking the country he will one day be head of. As a Pop at Eton William enjoyed the privilege of being allowed to chose his own waistcoats to complement his uniform. This one has the words "groovy baby" across the front of it.

Left:"Hello, all you groove jets out there. This is Tortel Love, and we are in the mood for some real groovin' here." DJ Will Windsor offers the modern royal alternative to his grandmother's traditional broadcasts.

Now well into her eighth decade, she is finally being applauded for being chic. The outfits she wore for her Golden Jubilee celebrations were a notable success. The French Magazine *L'Express* lauded her as the epitome of cool and quoted the designer Miuccia Prada's comment that the Queen "is truly one of the most elegant women in the world".

While the young Queen was never overly interested in her appearance her sister Princess Margaret dominated the world stage during the late 1940s and early 1950s. According to her biographer, Theo Aronson, "The princess's emergence into public life coincided, very happily, with a dramatic change in women's fashions, and in the years ahead she was to earn a reputation as one of the most stylishly dressed women of her generation." When Margaret adopted Christian Dior's "New Look" in the autumn of 1947 her stylish, tight-waisted, full skirts and new lower hemline were immediately imitated, says another writer, by "ten million British women". By 1956, and at the age of twenty-six, she was joint second with the Duchess of Windsor in the New York Dress Institute's list of the world's best-dressed women, the two of them being just beaten to the number one spot by the actress Grace Kelly.

William doesn't have to skip too many generations to find male ancestors with similar success in the fashion stakes. According to Princess Margaret, "My father (George VI) was very elegant. He had such a good figure for clothes and wore them beautifully." The King was happy spending hours at his tailors Benson and Clegg, where he tried on suits, discussed various styles and selected an appropriate cloth for each design.

His father, George V, had conservative taste in clothes, whether formal or informal, but according to his biographer, "they were to him an absorbing topic of conversation", and he once said that he belonged to a generation that was apt to judge a person's morals by the cut or fit of their suit. He wouldn't have had to judge for long

Below: With a practised wave at the crowds, William proves that he knows how to behave in the minefield of protocol and formality that surrounds the royal family. The traditional suit suggests that he is yet to discover his own style.

Right: August 1997 and the pin-up prince is emerging. William at fifteen looks relaxed with casual trousers and sleeves rolled up in this photo session in Scotland. As an adult he has so far resisted the traditional kilt that his father always wears when he stays at the Balmoral estate.

when it came to his eldest son, the future Edward VIII, whose suits and morals were both way ahead of their time. As king and, later, as Duke of Windsor, Edward showed "extraordinary interest in clothes", according to his biographer Frances Donaldson. Over the years Edward helped to popularize, among other things, soft-collared shirts, plus fours, bright jackets, loud check patterns for men and the dinner-jacket which, thanks to his influence, eventually superseded "white tie" for formal wear.

Thirty years after Princess Margaret gave drab, post-war Britain a much-needed splash of glamour, the diverging paths of royalty and fashion were reunited when Diana, Princess of Wales, was launched on to the public stage. While Margaret was a princess by birth, Diana had to make the leap from obscurity to fame almost overnight and at the same time learn how to dress and appear as a princess. This was far from easy, as she later

Left: Looking sophisticated at nineteen, William hosts a charity dinner at Highgrove in the absence of the Prince of Wales who had suffered a riding accident earlier in the day. Holding a glass of champagne, he follows supermodel Claudia Schiffer as they prepare to mix with other guests outside in the garden. The tousled hairstyle is a welcome contrast to his conformist black tie outfit.

recalled. "On the day we got engaged I literally had one long dress, one silk shirt, one smart pair of shoes and that was it. Suddenly my mother and I had to go and buy six of everything. We bought as much as we thought we needed but we still didn't have enough." After that she asked for help from Anna Harvey, then fashion editor of *Vogue*, where both Diana's sisters had worked. This gave her the confidence to pursue her own ideas. "Once I got established names like Victor Edelstein and Catherine Walker I could do it myself – ring them up and talk to them ... I had to find a niche where I was happy with the designer and what I required." Three years after her marriage a panel of twenty American fashion editors named Diana "The world's most influential woman in fashion today".

If Diana was "the most influential woman" William became the most influential baby. Diana followed royal tradition and purchased her son's clothes from The White House in London's Bond Street, which had dressed three generations of royal babies. In an early public appearance he was photographed wearing a blue and white smocked romper suit with puffed sleeves. The outfit was criticized in the newspapers as outdated and the sort of children's wear that his father would have worn. However, young British mothers thought otherwise and there was a sudden demand for plain romper suits in the same style. In Derbyshire a factory that had closed

Right: We shouldn't keep meeting like this! 27 June 2002 and Ms Schiffer presents William with the Porcelanosa Cup after his team won a charity polo match at Ashe Park in Hampshire.

seventeen months earlier was re-opened to create such suits, giving employment to dozens of machinists. Another early fashion success was a navy blue jumpsuit worn for a Kensington Palace photoshoot when he was eighteen months old. The padded suit, with its red elastic cuffs and red buttons and the letters ABC embroidered on the left shoulder, was simple, practical and fun, and won widespread approval.

By the time he became a teenager in 1995, William was beginning to develop two distinctive styles. Thanks to the influence of Diana, who tried to give him as normal an upbringing as possible, William loved designer trainers, Benetton T-shirts, black jeans and bomber jackets for when "off duty". Whether he was on the ski slopes at Klosters, buying a burger at McDonald's or queuing for a white-knuckle ride at Alton Towers, William looked the same as anyone his age – a distinct plus-point for the media-shy,

reserved prince. The second style was the formal royal look that generally emphasized class and status rather than personality. From his christening in August 1982 when he wore the Honiton lace robes made for the baptism of Queen Victoria's eldest daughter Vicky in 1841, through to the funerals of his mother and great-grandmother and the Golden Jubilee celebrations, William would have to dress in a style befitting a British prince. At the age of six he attended his first Trooping the Colour ceremony in a maroon suit with a shirt and blue tie. At the age of eight he again looked uncomfortably mature in a navy blue blazer and charcoal-coloured trousers as he joined his parents for a day of royal engagements in Cardiff to mark St David's

Below: William showing understated elegance as he leaves St Mary's church in Swansea amid a sea of robes and uniforms. The thanksgiving service was to mark the Queen's Golden Jubilee and his tie was a subtle compliment to his grandmother.

Right: Top hat and tails for the stylish prince who sensibly opts to carry rather than wear his top hat as he prepares to greet guests at a garden party at the Palace of Holyroodhouse, his grandmother's official royal residence in Scotland.

Day. For the Victory in Japan Day anniversary celebrations in August 1995 the same style of blazer with three gold buttons at the cuff looked elegant with cream-coloured chinos, but the Turnbull and Asser shirt that he was wearing, complete with gold cufflinks at his wrists, appeared far too dated for a teenager.

Left: July 1999 and, as guests arrive for lunch before the Cartier International Polo Tournament at Windsor, socialite Victoria Aitken discovers just who she is sitting next to. The wrap-around sunglasses are not particularly useful indoors, but at seventeen it's critical to look cool.

At fifteen, and just over 185 centimetres (6 feet) tall, William looked suave in a black dinner jacket at the London premier of *Spiceworld,* and at twenty he looked at ease in a frock coat at the garden party at Edinburgh's Holyroodhouse. Whenever the Queen is present at a public appearance William, Harry, Peter Phillips and all the other royal males are expected to wear a dark suit, shirt and tie, whether they are attending church or watching polo. When he attends his first state banquet William will need to wear white tie and, one day, if he serves in the armed forces, he will be expected to attend any major event from Trooping the Colour to Remembrance Sunday wearing full military uniform.

It was because William managed to look good in both formal and informal clothes that he began to receive plaudits from fashion editors and designers. When only fourteen he was listed among the best-dressed people of 1996 by the American *People* magazine because "He looks and dresses like a model. He makes no mistakes." At fifteen he topped the annual International Best-Dressed Poll, beating David Bowie, actor Rupert Everett and Tony Blair. The poll, founded by New York fashion publicist Eleanor Lambert in 1940, is a consensus of written ballots by 1,500 fashion journalists and designers. The final selection committee stated, "Prince William has shown extraordinary personal style and inspired a fresh, younger classicism among Savile Row tailors, thus influencing world fashion." Amazingly he managed all this influence while revising for his GCSEs and making only the rarest of public appearances. William's career as a US fashion icon shows no sign of abating. In the year his mother was declared "the best dressed person of all time" by *People* magazine to mark the millennium, William was praised for "jazzing up traditional Savile Row suits one minute, while donning sneakers and baseball cap the next which has helped him to become a style-setter of the young set".

William's influence as a fashion icon/superstar became apparent in July 1999 at the Cartier polo tournament in Windsor Great Park. William, dressed in a blazer and dark blue trousers, innocently donned a pair of wraparound sunglasses. The effect was immediate. Nearly every British newspaper picked up on the story. *The Sunday Times* asked a colour psychologist, who advises Shell and Mothercare, to give her opinion of the colour of the frames, the *Mirror* featured a psychologist from Warwick University discussing what your choice of sunglasses reveals about your personality, and *The Times* later joined in with an article on how sales of the five main wraparound designs had soared since William had worn them.

Unlike his father, who prefers Savile Row tailors such as Anderson and Shepherd, William has been known to shop at Burberry for blazers and jumpers. The camel-coloured sweater he wore over a pair of jeans at a Highgrove presscall earned him a nomination on the *People* 2001 best-dressed list. William is not averse to logos and brand names and has worn Ralph Lauren shirts, Tenson jackets and Columbia pants for skiing.

Although William has to toe the royal line when it comes to fashion, as he gets older he seems more than willing to rock the boat a little and, like his mother, he knows his own mind. Diana famously upstaged the Queen at the 1984 State Opening of Parliament by wearing her hair up in an elaborate design, or at least that was how the papers chose to interpret it the following day. William hasn't gone to any drastic lengths yet, but there are signs that he will shy away from royal formality. For instance, he is happy to sport the three gold, copper and leather bracelets that he bought on a tour of Botswana, first spotted in the spring of 1999 at the christening of his godson Konstantin of Greece at the Greek Church in Bayswater, west London. Another minor act of rebellion was to turn up at the 2001 Braemar Games, stubbornly refusing to wear a kilt. All of his royal relations, including his mother, have at some time attended the games wearing tartan. William's insistence on wearing a navy blue suit was again pounced on by the newspapers, prompting headlines such as "Too Cool For A Kilt".

When he was a Pop at Eton, he revealed, "I've always liked the uniform, particularly the Pop uniform, which allows you to wear your own waist-

Above: September 2000 and there is nothing stilted about this photoshoot. William opts for jeans and a beige sweater with the Burberry logo on as he poses for photographs to mark the start of his gap year travels. The denims prove he's a typical youth, but the designer top offers a touch of class.

coats, and the stick-ups (stiff wing collar) and tie." The Union Jack waist-coat he wore for a photoshoot in 1999 was particularly daring.

William does not seek media attention through his fashion sense. He is on record as saying, "I just want to be ordinary." Sadly his status, good looks and warm personality combine to make this virtually impossible.

Right: Exactly a year later William adopts the student look for his first day at St Andrews. Unlike his father who, at the height of the swinging sixties, arrived at Cambridge University wearing a jacket and tie, William looks casual and ready to fit in.

CHAPTER SEVEN

WILLIAM AND SPORT

His father has tried everything from parachuting to deep-sea diving and his mother was a keep-fit fanatic who loved swimming. His brother has said that he would love to be a professional polo player and his aunt joined the three-day eventing team at the 1976 Olympics. Grandad still enjoys carriage driving even in his eighties and Granny goes riding every weekend at Windsor. It's hardly surprising that with a sports-loving pedigree as strong as the royal family's, William has developed into a creditable swimmer, footballer, skier, polo player, rugby player and huntsman.

Life behind royal doors is protected, cushioned and totally unlike the lives of most of William's contemporaries, so it is not surprising that William is attracted to sports and pastimes that are exciting and often dangerous. William's latest passion is for motorbike riding, which makes his father "frantic with worry". Charles had hoped that the sporty VW Golf that he bought him for his seventeenth birthday would take his son's mind off motorbikes, but within a year William was tearing around the family estate on his Kawasaki. Charles knows that motorbikes are twenty times more dangerous than cars, but he also knows that when William has decided to do something there is no point trying to stop him.

Right: Nearly all the members of the royal family are addicted to sport. They realize early on that, in areas such as polo, you generally succeed on merit rather than birth, a welcome relief after the constant obsequiousness they are faced with in their day-to-day lives. The Princess Royal once said, "The horse is the only one who doesn't know I'm royal."

Left: In the summer of 1992 the ten year old William's early passion for motor-racing was fuelled by a visit to the Grand Prix track at Silverstone where he was given a guided tour by former champions Jackie Stewart and Nigel Mansell.

Motorbikes might not be to the Queen's liking but horses obviously are and William's love of hunting and polo gets a hearty thumbs up from his royal relations. "At Windsor weekends", says one horse-hating former courtier, "there is no talk except about the horse. They ride it, race it, drive it and bang on about it incessantly from morning till night. If you know nothing and care even less about the horse, you're useless." William has obviously caught the Windsor bug. Each winter, when his studies allow, he joins the Beaufort Hunt near Highgrove. The prince usually joins the hunt midway to avoid the photographers and other onlookers who gather at the start of the meet.

William took up hunting seriously in October 1999 when he joined his father at the Beaufort Hunt. There was predictable criticism from organizations such as the League Against Cruel Sports, which accused Charles of trying to make "a political statement" by encouraging his son to take part on the very first day of the foxhunting season. A spokeswoman for the prince robustly defended the decision. "Hunting is still a legal sport", she said, "and everybody knows that the Prince of Wales is a hunter. As for the

Below: Naturally at home in the world of hunting, nine-year-old William receives an affectionate welcome from the Beaufort hounds while on a visit to Badminton House in Gloucestershire in April 1991. Harry and their distant cousin Lady Gabriella Windsor await their turn.

Above: November 1999 and the seventeen-year-old Prince is at long last able to ride with the Beaufort Hunt, an outing that resulted in a rare barrage of criticism for the prince from journalists and opponents of hunting. Typically independent, William wore his own tweed jacket instead of the traditional "blue and buff" hunt uniform.

boys, while it is still legal they are perfectly free to make their own choice." The same week a family friend admitted, "In presentation terms it might have been better if William had not gone out, but he is a young man with his own opinions. Hell would have to freeze over before he could have been talked out of hunting yesterday." Despite his strong convictions William knew that there was no possibility of his being able to march in the countryside "March for Liberty and Livelihood", which took place in London in September 2002. Charles did give his Highgrove staff paid leave to attend the event but William was confined to watching the march from the rooftops of St James's Palace.

Hunting has been part of the royal way of life for generations. Prince Albert rode "boldly and hard" with the hounds, according to Queen Victoria. Their daughter-in-law, the future Queen Alexandra, cut an elegant figure riding side-saddle in her velvet habit and silk hat. Alexandra's son George V rode frequently, often accompanied by his sons, and before she was married the Queen Mother also hunted. Surprisingly in recent years the only members of the royal family who have never hunted are the Queen and Prince Philip.

Hunting is also part of William's Spencer heritage. The Pytchley hunt was established in 1756 by the prince's ancestor the first Earl Spencer. William's aunt Lady Sarah McCorquodale often used to ride with Prince Charles at the Meynell Hunt. Diana was never a fan of the sport, although she did occasionally follow the riders by Land Rover. "The princess does not like riding", said a member of the household in the late 1980s, "but she has made a marvellous effort with the children. The boys do a lot of riding at Highgrove and they are pretty proficient."

Charles took up hunting only at the age of twenty-six after being coached in the basics at Windsor by Princess Anne. Charles admitted, "Quite a lot

of the time I was petrified", while his fearless sister "used to hurtle past me, galloping flat out." Charles encouraged William and Harry to go out with the junior Beaufort during their half term break in the autumn of 1990 when William was eight and Harry six. Four years later he introduced them to the art of cubbing – the pursuit of fox cubs to prepare horses and hounds for the season.

Philip is no doubt proud that his grandson has taken up what used to be his favourite sport – polo – a hobby that Philip was introduced to by "Uncle Dickie", Earl Mountbatten of Burma. It is also, of course, the favourite hobby of William's own father. Both William and Harry had been playing for a couple of years before they finally teamed up with Charles in his maroon and blue Highgrove colours for a match against the local side at Cirencester Park Polo Club. Dubbed the "blue-blooded dream team", the three princes are now attracting more people to the sport.

Polo may be a popular royal sport, but shooting has even wider appeal for the Windsors, with nearly every royal male taking part and every royal female acting as a "picker-up" of the birds. The royal family spends each Christmas at Sandringham, in Norfolk, which another queen – Victoria –

Above: An all-round athlete, William has tried his hand at most sports, including this early attempt at rowing along the River Thames from the boathouse at Eton, 18 April 1996.

described as "rather wild-looking flat, bleak country". There William takes part in the traditional Boxing Day shoot. He also makes occasional weekend visits for shoots in the autumn. Prince Philip invited William and a group of his friends to stay for a weekend in November 2001 and it is an encouraging sign for the duke that his grandson has inherited an affection not only for the sport but also for the countryside in general.

Shooting, like hunting, spans the royal generations. George VI recorded in 1945 that his nineteen-year-old daughter "Lilibet" – the Queen – shot her first pheasant. Two years later, besides countless tiaras and necklaces, the King gave his daughter "a pair of Purdey guns". The Queen doesn't shoot any more, but Charles does, and he always uses his grandfather's Purdey, which was passed on to him by the Queen Mother.

A typical day's shoot can bring in a bag of several hundred birds. At the Boxing Day shoot in 2000 William spent four-and-a-half hours outside with Prince Philip, Harry and Peter Phillips, and the group brought down a record number of birds. One onlooker said, "He and Peter Phillips stuck together most of the day. William seemed particularly happy and looked as if he was really enjoying himself. Virtually every time he aimed, he brought down a bird."

As with hunting, William has come under constant scrutiny from those opposed to blood sports. Many people feel that had Diana lived the princes would have followed a different path. The critics fail to recognize that Diana was brought up in this environment just as much as Charles was. In fact, the two of them met at a shooting party in a muddy field in the Silver Jubilee year of 1977. Diana's father and grandfather joined the royal shoots, and her maternal grandfather Lord Fermoy had enjoyed a fine day's shooting with George VI the day before the King died at Sandringham in February 1952.

To celebrate William starting at St Andrews, Charles gave him one of the finest guns in the world so that he could

Right: Holidays are a chance to try new forms of exercise. Here, in July 1997, the prince enjoys jet-skiing while staying in St Tropez with Harry and Diana. This turned out to be their last holiday together before the princess's death.

pursue his other passion – deer stalking. The gun, which was handmade in Scotland, was reputed to have cost nearly £20,000. It has a stock of highly prized Turkish walnut, as well as being engraved with a special motif and inlaid with gold. It is a full-bore .243-calibre sporting rifle and can provide a skilled shot. William shot his first deer when he was fourteen. Once again there was criticism in the press and rumours of a rift in the family until Diana stepped in to disclose that she had not fallen out with her son for taking part in the sport.

At Eton, William enjoyed a variety of sports, from rowing to rugby, all of them safely uncontroversial. His mother would have been delighted that William was appointed captain of Eton's swimming team in 1999 – a position that entailed organizing galas and training younger boys. His duties also involved keeping records of swimming events and welcoming visiting teams. At seventeen he was reckoned by the press to be one of Britain's top one hundred 50-metre free-stylers in his age group.

Diana was a keen swimmer and taught William the basics when he was a child. They often swam together during the summer breaks, the last time

Below: Both Charles and Diana adored skiing and enjoyed teaching their two sons the basic techniques on the nursery slopes. Dogged by the paparazzi, the royal party eventually learned to strike a bargain with the press by posing for photographs each morning. While Harry coped well with the pleasure, William – as here – found it more difficult to deal with.

Right: William is an
average skier, happy to
leave the daredevil stunts
to Harry. Since the death
of Diana, the princes no
longer visit the resort of
Lech, preferring their
father's favourite
destination, Klosters.

being July 1997, a month before Diana's death, when they holidayed in the Mediterranean on Mohammed Al Fayed's yacht *Jonikal*. William is a powerful swimmer and in July 1999 he was selected as part of a three-man team to join three hundred others for a weekend triathlon held at the Welsh port of Fishguard. He was spotted diving into the harbour, dressed in a wetsuit, for the first leg of the competition, a 1,500-metre swim, where by all accounts he ploughed through the water to come a creditable second. Racing under the pseudonym of Tristram, William opted out of the presentation ceremony later in the day and left the glory of winning first place to his team mates "Jim" and "John".

William also enjoyed learning water polo at Eton, a sport that he has taken up again at St Andrews, practising in the local swimming pool. With his blond hair hidden under a swimming cap and his eyes shielded by

Left: For someone in the solitary position of a prince, William has adapted well to team sports. Here, as captain of the "Gaileys" team, named after his housemaster, William and his team take on "Hursts" in the semi-final of the inter-house tournament, played on the legendary playing fields of Eton.

goggles, it would be hard to recognize him as the country's number one pin-up which, of course, is exactly what he hopes for. In May 2002 he was awarded his sports colours after his first season in the university water polo team. This time he was listed as William Wales and was one of fifteen members of the squad to receive colours.

William has played, and supported, rugby from an early age. At Ludgrove he was rugby and hockey team captain as well as representing the school in cross-country running. In his early teens his mother took him by train from Paddington to Cardiff to watch the Welsh team in action and he has often been seen on the terraces with his hat pulled low over his brow as a disguise. In February 2002, on the day after Princess Margaret's funeral, he was spotted at Twickenham cheering England to victory over Ireland in rugby's Six Nations Championship.

It is also rugby that has enabled him to join the royal list of sporting injuries. When he was sixteen he broke a finger on his left hand while playing rugby at Eton. This was as embarrassing as it was painful since it meant that he had to have his arm in a sling during his first solo public appearance when he became godfather to Prince Konstantine Alexios, grandson of the exiled king of Greece.

William's other love is football, a sport that has been more or less abandoned by the royal family since the Queen handed the World Cup to Bobby Moore in 1966. It is not William's affection for the sport that intrigues the media, but why exactly he supports Aston Villa. William has so far given no clues as to why he supports the Birmingham side rather than a London club such as Harry's favourite team, Arsenal. Vinnie Jones, once known as the hard man of soccer and now an actor, tried to prise the secret out of William at the Press Complaints Commission's tenth birthday party, but the answer was an evasive, "It just happened that way".

William always wears the team's claret and blue hat and scarf whenever he watches the Midlands team playing, and he even wore the woolly hat at his father's fiftieth birthday party. Four years later the soccer-mad prince was spotted knocking a football around with friends after a polo match while managing to have a conversation with a friend on his mobile phone at the same time. The bookmakers William Hill immediately gave odds of 500–1 that William would one day play for

Below: A manly thump for the opposition as "Hursts" beat "Gaileys" 2–1. Happy to don the blue and fawn team colours, William clearly couldn't be bothered to track down matching socks.

Aston Villa at a professional level and of 1,000–1 that he will play for England in Euro 2004.

Having galvanized bookmakers into giving odds that he'll be the next David Beckham, William threw a spanner into the works six weeks later when it was revealed that he plays golf for hours on end. A royal insider revealed, "His new obsession has taken us all by surprise, as football used to be his passion." Of course, in the press, royals aren't allowed to do anything by halves and so by the following morning the tabloids proclaimed, "William to be the new Tiger Woods!"

It helps the privacy-loving prince that his granny has two golf courses – one at Windsor, the other at Balmoral – as well as a swimming pool at Buckingham Palace and thousands of acres of woodland in Norfolk and moorland in Scotland for shooting and stalking in almost total seclusion. One day he will own all of these, but at present he can forget the pressures of royal life – at least for most of the time – while he revels in being a sportsman – the role he probably enjoys most of all. It is also a comfort for the man who will one day occupy the loneliest of positions that he can blend into so many team sports as just another player.

Previous pages: One of the favourite sports of royalty, William and Harry enjoy an exhilarating polo match. The princes continue the tradition of their grandfather and father, who are both passionate about the game.

Right: In polo players have to pass the ball using their right hands, a challenge for the left-handed prince, seen here playing for the Ronnie Wallace Memorial Trophy at the Beaufort Club in July 2002.

Left: Dubbed "the blue-blooded dream team", Charles, William and Harry, with the help of a fourth player, formed their own Highgrove team. They are seen here at Cirencester Polo Club wearing the distinctive maroon and blue shirts.

CHAPTER EIGHT

WILLIAM AND THE MEDIA

Shortly before her death, the Princess of Wales told Tina Brown, editor of *The New Yorker*, "All my hopes are on William now. I try to din it into him about the media – the dangers and how he must understand and handle it. It's too late for the rest of the family. But William, I think he has it." The "it" that Diana thought William had at the age of only fifteen was the ability to recognize the pressures and pitfalls of a life under constant media scrutiny. "I think he has it," could also be taken to mean that in his mother's eyes William had, like her, the star quality that would prove magnetic to press and public alike.

Since his early teens when it became apparent that William was growing into the male equivalent of Diana, tall, blond, athletic and with a blemish-free skin, a host of grateful media moguls were ready and waiting. Aged only thirteen, William moved seamlessly from cute prince to heart-throb when he was splashed across the pages of teen magazine *Smash Hits*. "We had some reader interest," the editor, Kate Thornton, recalled. "We'd been sitting around thinking, 'He's quite a good-looking lad and has potential as a pin-up.'"

The *Smash Hits* pull-out of a blue-blazered William generated such high sales that in May 1996 the magazine went a step farther and offered "I Love Willy" stickers, which sent

Right: Relaxed and charming, William has inherited his mother's ability to mix easily with people of all ages and all backgrounds. Here William meets volunteers from the Prince's Trust at the Lighthouse, a centre for architecture and design in Glasgow, September 2001.

Left: William, or 'Wombat' as his father called him at the time, celebrates his second birthday at Kensington Palace with a press photocall. The intrigued prince gives a cautious peek at the newly recorded film footage of him playing in the family garden.

the sales even higher to 250,000. The *Sun* picked up the story, declaring William a "smasher". William was soon hot news in the teen market with the teen magazine, *Live and Kicking*, joining the fray with "Top Ten Reasons Why Wills is Cool". Reason number 3 was "He knows how to par-tee!", number 6 was "He wears trainers instead of sensible shoes", and at number 7 was "He's not scared of going on scary theme park rides!" Editor Jeremy Mark felt that William's fans "see him as a regular boy growing up in Britain." Perhaps more worrying for William was Mark's other com-

Left: Diana's silver leek brooch and the daffodil buttonholes provide a clue. 1 March 1991, St David's Day, and the future Prince of Wales makes his first visit to the principality with his mother. Here they prepare to greet members of a youth orchestra who have played in their honour.

ment: "A lot of our readers find the idea of being a princess exciting and glamorous." Later on fifty-four Valentine cards winged their way to William at Eton. This was apparently an increase of fifty-three over the previous year when only his mother had bothered to send one.

With younger generations consistently the most anti-monarchy in the polls, William's appeal to a new generation is vital in maintaining the royal family's popularity in the twenty-first century. A survey in *The People* newspaper put William second in the list of "100 men and women set to dominate the new millennium".

Two surveys in 2002 showed that William's appeal spans the generations. In July he topped a poll to find the "smoothest" ladies' man, with fifty-one per cent of the votes – far ahead of his nearest rival, the current Bond actor, Pierce Brosnan. At the other end of the chronological scale a survey of under-tens held in the spring of that year by Premier Christian Radio decided that William should definitely marry Britney Spears.

William is also in popular demand in other areas of the media. When in the late autumn of 2000 ITN cameraman Eugene Campbell spent three days filming William on his Raleigh International project in southern Chile, ITV decided at short notice to show a half-hour special, *Prince William in Chile,* at 8 p.m. on 11 December. The BBC immediately ordered a last-minute change to its peak-time schedule and screened its *Prince William Special* at 7.30 p.m., using the ITN footage that UK broadcasting rules compelled it to share.

William undoubtedly has his mother's star quality but he also has his father's sceptical and often self-deprecating attitude to life in the media spotlight. While many teenagers would have revelled in the attention of the latest teen magazines as well as tabloid coverage, William, certainly during the *Smash Hits* phase, cringed at all the polls and posters and his relationship with the media in the following years was volatile.

Royal distrust of the press is nothing new. Two centuries ago George III, outraged at being constantly misreported in the newspapers, appointed a court newsman to ensure that they printed an accurate court circular. The position remained more or less the same throughout successive reigns, evolving slowly into the office of press secretary that exists today.

The Queen's attitude to the media is ambivalent. According to one of her biographers, Brian Hoey, "'She wants harmony, peace and a quiet life – the media demand headlines, soundbites and scandal." The Queen realizes that in and around the saturation coverage of royal marriages, affairs, divorces and court cases, there is also the continual and vital coverage of the serious work of monarchy, from state visits to Christmas broadcasts. Without photoshoots, interviews and documentaries the royal family wouldn't be accessible to the public and interest in the monarchy would stagnate. Prince Charles admitted this, albeit jokingly, when he told a group of journalists, "It's when you characters don't want to photograph me that I have to worry."

The member of the royal family who had the most positive media profile was the Queen Mother, who masterminded her own public relations for nearly eighty years. After the announcement of her engagement to the Duke of York, second son of George V, she poured her heart out to an enterprising journalist from *The Star,* who knocked at the door of her parents' London home. All future in-depth interviews were banned – a rule that she maintained for the rest of her life. She did however co-operate successfully with photographers from Cecil Beaton down to the pushiest of paparazzi. She was labelled "the last great silent star", and what she chose not to communicate verbally she more than made up for visually. After she became Queen in 1936 she actively used the media to promote the image of a happy family life. There were regular photoshoots of the couple with their two daughters. During the war the King and Queen were shown touring bombed cities, offering words of sympathy and showing the defiant charm that led Hitler to call Elizabeth "the most dangerous woman in Europe."

William has developed a similar relationship with the media. He isn't quite a "silent star" but there are some similarities between the Hollywood

Above: A taste of things to come. William wearing black tie for the first time in public makes his way through a blitz of camera flashes as he joins Charles and Harry at the charity premier of the Spice Girl movie *Spiceworld*. The outing in December 1997 was intended as a treat for the boys, coming just three months after the death of Diana.

studio system of the 1930s and 1940s and the way the offices of St James's Palace operate. Just as film fans were given carefully controlled set pieces of Cary Grant and Spencer Tracey fishing, driving or learning their lines, so seventy years later photographers and cameramen are offered themed photoshoots, showing William skiing, teaching children to read in Chile or beginning his academic life at St Andrews. In return for first-class shots in varied locations, the British media have agreed to leave him in peace the rest of the time.

William has been under media scrutiny almost since his birth. At thirty-six hours of age he faced nearly three hundred photographers, journalists, and cameramen from Britain, Europe, the US and Japan, all fighting for a slice of pavement opposite the entrance to the hospital's Lindo Wing. At nine months of age the prince was reintroduced to the British press during a photocall at Government House in Auckland during his parents' tour of New Zealand. As he crawled and gurgled across a blanket the world heard Charles call him by his nickname of "Wills" and saw a proud Diana help him to stand up on shaky legs for the benefit of the cameras.

When he was eighteen months old there was another photoshoot in his parents' private garden at Kensington Palace. By the time a similar one was devised for his second birthday he was becoming unfazed by the cameras and peered down the viewfinder of an ITN camera to see his own image on tape. Charles used this as an early warning lesson for his son. Pointing out a boom microphone on one of the television cameras he jokingly told Wills, "Those are the big sausage-things which record every-thing you say – start learning!" The growing media fascination with the tiniest Windsor was reflected in the following morning's newspapers when every tabloid faithfully recorded that William was now nearly 90 cen-timetres (three feet) high, weighed almost 13 kilograms (28 pounds) and could say "Dadda", "Daddy", "ball" and "ant".

If anyone understands what it is like to grow up under the media spot-light it is the Queen. Before she was ten Elizabeth's cherubic features appeared on china, chocolate boxes and children's magazines. Hospital wards were named after her, as well as a slice of Antarctica that is still known as Princess Elizabeth Land. A popular song was dedicated to her and her face appeared on a six-cent stamp in Newfoundland. In her early youth it seems to have had an adverse effect on her. According to Lady Helen Graham, one of her mother's ladies-in-waiting, "She could not understand why photographers would pick her out for attention and frowned upon them with obvious disapproval."

Several times during William's life the Queen has stepped in to voice her concern over the treatment that he is experiencing. In recent years she has denounced the memoirs by Patrick Jephson and Ken Wharfe. She was also desperately concerned during 2002 about the possible repercussions for William and Harry as more and more personal details about Diana emerged during the trial of the former butler Paul Burrell.

As he grew from being a child to a teenager William, too, showed obvi-ous disapproval when he was being photographed. Photography has developed considerably since the Queen's youth, and ever larger zoom lenses, creating ever better-quality images, could snap the young prince swimming off isolated beaches, playing football with his friends at school or watching shoots at Sandringham or Balmoral. On his first skiing trip to Lech in the spring of 1991 when he was only eight he ducked out of a pho-tocall of his first skiing lesson, telling his mother's detective, "I feel sick". He was escorted back to the Arlberg hotel looking close to tears as he walked hand-in-hand with another detective. The next day a UK tabloid newspaper led with the story "Wills the Wimp", together with a photo-graph captioned "Cry baby".

Much of William's attitude to the media has been shaped by the way the press treated his mother. Di-mania began in the run-up to her marriage when even respectable photographers stalked her each day on the way to work and followed her every public appearance. The wedding, the births of William and Harry, Diana's undoubted glamour and her love of designer clothes all added fuel to the fire so that media interest in her never waned. It was estimated that a photograph of Diana on the cover of a magazine guaranteed an increase in circulation of between twenty and twenty-five per cent, so it was obviously in the interests of the press to keep real and invented stories about her in constant circulation.

After his parents' separation William witnessed the press harrassment of his mother at first hand. On a trip to a West End cinema in 1993, Diana suddenly rounded on a photographer outside and yelled, "You make my life hell!" before prodding him in the chest and pointing a finger in his face.

Incidents like these prompted Diana's temporary withdrawal from public life, which she announced at a charity lunch in December 1993. "When I began my public life twelve years ago," she told the hushed audience, "I understood that the media might be interested in what I did ... But I was not aware of how overwhelming that attention would become; nor the extent to which it would affect both my public duties and my personal life, in a manner that has been hard to bear."

While William and Harry have never wavered in their defence of Diana's reputation both before and since her death, many of her staff, friends and associates have pointed out that Diana was unafraid to use the media to suit her own ends. They argue that she was responsible for many leaks and tip-offs that would result in photographers turning up when she was on so-called private visits, even when she was with her sons.

Unlike Diana, William refused to fight battles with the media and, whenever possible, avoided being photographed. In August 1996, at a pre-arranged photocall at Balmoral, William gave only the occasional glance at the cameras, leaving the relaxed posing to Charles and twelve-year-old Harry, who has never shared William's reticence with the press.

To protect William when he started at Eton in September 1995 the Press Complaints Commission appealed to editors to respect the thirteen-year-

Left: 7 February 2001 and Charles and William pause on the way into a party at London's Somerset House to mark the tenth anniversary of the Press Complaints Commission. They were joined a few minutes later by Camilla Parker Bowles, the first time all three had been present at an official public engagement.

old prince's privacy. "He is not an institution; nor a soap star; nor a football hero", Lord Wakeham pointed out. "He is a child: in the next few years, perhaps the most important and painful of his life, he will grow up and become a man." Few, including Lord Wakeham, could have realized just how painful the next few years would be. The presence of photographers roaring through Paris on that night in August 1997 was one of several factors that combined to cause the fatal crash. There was a great deal of analysis in the press to the effect that if William had such terrible insecurities about them before Diana's death he would never again be able to cope with a life in the glare of the media. They were to be proved wrong.

In the immediate aftermath of Diana's death, the media began to analyze and redefine their attitude to public figures. A chastened UK press agreed not to use intrusive photographs and to refuse to buy any paparazzi shots from agencies. At the same time the Queen, Prince Charles and other members of the royal family took steps to try to improve relations with the media. Press receptions were reintroduced on foreign tours and occasionally the press were invited to share the same aircraft as the royal family.

The first sign that William was beginning to adjust to the ever-present cameras came just over six months after Diana's death when Charles,

Below: 29 September
2000 and scribbling
journalists make a note of
William's every comment
as he uses a pre-arranged
photocall at Highgrove to
condemn a recent
biography of Diana by her
former private secretary.
Also facing the group is
Charles's press secretary
Colleen Harris (wearing a
white pashmina shawl),
keeping a watchful eye
on the media.

William and Harry arrived in Vancouver during the visit when Wills-mania first became apparent. At first William looked aghast at the public adulation but as the day progressed he began to relax. At the end of the visit, all three princes were given Canadian Winter Olympics bomber jackets and caps. Charles took the lead and put his team cap on backwards. Harry slipped into his jacket and cap and then William tried his on. To the delight of the crowd he also put his cap on backwards and then gestured with his hands and arms like a rap star.

Three months later William marked his first birthday since the death of his mother by agreeing to be interviewed by the Press Association and revealed that he finds it difficult to cope with the adulation of fans. On a more positive note he revealed how much he liked sport, reading, action films, and the company of his black Labrador, Widgeon.

In July 1999, shortly before his driving test, photographers were invited to Highgrove for a staged shot of William driving with L-plates before

Below: 29 September 2000 and scribbling journalists make a note of William's every comment as he uses a pre-arranged photocall at Highgrove to condemn a recent biography of Diana by her former private secretary. Also facing the group is Charles's press secretary Colleen Harris (wearing a white pashmina shawl), keeping a watchful eye on the media.

pulling up a safe distance away from his grinning father and brother. The following April the three princes once again posed for the cameras on a skiing holiday to Klosters. William even chatted to the press, describing his holiday so far as "good fun", and exchanging banter about Aston Villa's recent run of luck.

In the last few years William has proved himself more than capable of defending himself if he feels that he or his family are being unfairly treated. In July 1988 William and Harry issued a rare statement expressing their

Above: Totally relaxed and confident, William joins Charles for a joint visit to Glasgow in September 2001 and effortlessly takes centre stage.

unhappiness with a Sunday newspaper for revealing plans for a surprise fiftieth birthday party for Prince Charles later in the year. The newspaper said that princes would star in their own play alongside Emma Thompson and Stephen Fry. A spokeswoman for the princes said, "They are very disappointed that (the story) has got out after they kept it a secret for so long."

In September 2000, during a photocall to brief the press about his gap year, William voiced his concerns about another attack on the memory of his mother. This was a direct criticism of the book by Patrick Jephson. According to William his mother "continues to be exploited, and Harry and I regret that this is happening."

More regrets were expressed the following year when he arrived at St Andrews. The day after a photosession to document the prince's first day at college, all the photographers and news crews left, in line with a request from St James's Palace. The following day, William alerted Charles's staff to the presence of a lone film crew that was filming some of the university buildings. Embarrassingly for all concerned, the team were part of Prince Edward's Ardent Production Company and were filming for an American cable programme called *A-Z of Royalty*.

William knows that his every move will be documented for the rest of his life, and he knows from the bitter experience of his mother's life that this can, at any moment, escalate out of control. At the moment he is safe thanks to the support and affection generated for him after Diana's death. He also knows that he must maintain this status quo at all costs.

Overleaf: Head and shoulders above all other celebrities, William joins Prince Charles and the Queen on stage following the Party at the Palace to mark the Queen's Golden Jubilee, watched by, among others, Eric Clapton, Brian May, Sir Paul McCartney, Sir Cliff Richard, The Corrs, Tom Jones and Dame Shirley Bassey, 3 June 2002.

Right: Ignoring the cameras, video cameras and ever present security men, William looks totally at ease on a public walkabout during his first official visit to Scotland in September 2001.

CHAPTER NINE

COMING OF AGE

For some of William's royal relations reaching twenty-one proved to be a pivotal moment, not only for their immediate future but in some cases for the rest of their lives. At twenty-one the Queen married the man she loved while at the same age Princess Margaret began to fall in love with the man she would never be allowed to marry. Prince Charles was formally invested as Prince of Wales while Princess Anne won a gold medal for her country as well as a starring role in a children's television programme.

The previous Prince of Wales, the future Edward VIII, refused to celebrate his coming of age. The prince became twenty-one on 23 June 1915 when he was fighting with the army in France during the First World War. In a letter to a family friend, he revealed that his birthday "was a sad and depressing occasion, with this ghastly war on and so many of one's best friends killed. In fact I did my best to forget it altogether." The following month he spent his first night in the trenches. "My impressions that night were of constant close proximity to death, repugnance from the stink of the unburied corpses ... and general gloom and apprehension", he told his father George V, adding, "It was a real eye opener to me, now I have some slight conception of all that our officers and men have to go thro!! The whole thing is horrible and ghastly beyond comprehension."

Right: The pin-up prince at nineteen. William looks to the future as he arrives in Scotland to begin his four years as a student, September 2001.

Left: Shy and uncertain, the teenage Prince acknowledges the crowds. By the mid-1990s Di-mania had been superseded by Wills-mania as the crowds began to chant "We want William" whenever he appeared.

Edward's younger brother, the future George VI – William's great-grandfather – managed to obtain leave from the war to mark his twenty-first birthday the following year. Bertie, as he was known to his family, entered the world on 14 December 1895, much to everyone's alarm. The date was "Mausoleum Day", the thirty-fourth anniversary of the Prince Consort's death, which Queen Victoria insisted on spending in gloomy contemplation of the marble likeness over his tomb at Frogmore. Victoria wasted no time in telling the nervous parents she was "rather distressed that this happy event should have taken place on a darkly sad anniversary". Later, she conceded that the arrival "might be looked upon as a gift from God!" and intimated that she would be prepared to forgive everyone concerned if he was named after his great-grandfather.

During the First World War, Bertie served with the Royal Navy. Six months before his birthday he witnessed the Battle of Jutland from his post on HMS *Collingwood*, writing soon afterwards, "I feel very different now that I have seen a German ship filled with Germans and have seen it fired at with our guns. It was a great experience to have gone through and one not easily forgotten." He celebrated his twenty-first birthday at Buckingham Palace where his father invested him with the Order of the Garter, an order of chivalry that dated back to 1348 and which, according to one of his biographers was "the order for which he conceived a lifelong passion". "I cannot thank you enough for having made me a Knight of the Garter", he wrote to his father. "I feel very proud to have it, and will always try to live up to it." In 1948, as George VI, he reintroduced the annual procession of Garter Knights to St George's Chapel, Windsor, a tradition that his daughter the Queen still maintains.

For William's grandmother the months immediately before and after her twenty-first birthday were among the most memorable of

Below: A world away from reality. William's great-grandfather, the future King George VI, as Duke of York, in bowler hat and double-breasted suit, demonstrates how royalty dress for the helter-skelter to the evident amazement of a young onlooker.

Right: Three kings. The Queen's grandfather King George V is flanked by his two eldest sons, her uncle the future King Edward VIII on the left, and her father the future King George VI on the right. All of them would reign during the Abdication year of 1936, the only time in British history since 1485 when three kings have occupied the throne in one year.

her life. Princess Elizabeth is reckoned to have fallen in love with her distant cousin Lieutenant Philip Mountbatten during a visit by the royal family to the Royal Naval College at Dartmouth during the summer of 1939, when she was just thirteen. Despite her parents' efforts to introduce her to a variety of aristocrats nicknamed "the Bodyguard" by her grandmother Queen Mary, Elizabeth never wavered in her affection. According to the biographer Robert Lacey, "When in the late summer of 1946 at Balmoral, Prince Philip of Greece proposed directly to Princess Elizabeth, she ignored father, mother, King, Queen and government and accepted him there and then."

One problem was the long-planned tour of South Africa which would take the royal family away from Britain for four months. Elizabeth was told that that not only did her engagement not fit into the scheme of things, but that it should remain a secret until she returned in the summer of 1947. The royal family left a Britain battered by the worst winter of frosts and blizzards within living memory. They would not leave South Africa until 23 April, two days after Elizabeth's birthday, since it had been decided that it would be a fitting gesture if Elizabeth marked her coming of age in one of the dominions rather than at home.

Monday 21 April 1947 proved to be more of an endurance test than a celebration for Princess Elizabeth. To give the occasion as high a profile as possible, the South African government had earlier declared it a public holiday. That afternoon, accompanied only by a lady-in-waiting and an equerry, she took the salute at a march past of Cape Town's finest soldiers, veterans, nurses, civil defence volunteers and cadets. If that wasn't enough, she had to conduct the ceremony under the eye of Prime Minister Smuts, his cabinet, and the entire imperial and foreign diplomatic corps.

After the march past the princess drove to Rosebank for a rally of youth organizations. The in the evening, before attending two formal balls in her

Below: The Queen as Princess Elizabeth celebrated her twenty-first birthday during the royal tour of South Africa. Separated from the man she loved for three and a half months she found much of the visit an ordeal. When in February 1947 she was shown the final demanding programme she said sharply "Well, I hope we shall survive, that's all."

Above: Happy at last. At midnight on 8 July 1947 it was announced from Buckingham Palace that the King and Queen had "with the greatest pleasure" given their consent to the betrothal of their eldest daughter to Lieutenant Philip Mountbatten RN.

Right: Princess Margaret was the Diana of her day. Reckoned to have the most beautiful eyes in the world, the youngest daughter of King George VI regularly topped the polls as the best dressed woman in Britain.

honour she was required to broadcast her birthday message live to most of her father's 500 million subjects worldwide. Without faltering she called upon the whole empire to witness her solemn act of dedication. "It is very simple," she said calmly and resolutely, "I declare before you all that my whole life, whether it be long or short, shall be devoted to your service and the service of our great Imperial Commonwealth to which we all belong ... God help me to make good my vow; and God bless all of you who are willing to share in it." Thirty years later, after her Silver Jubilee Thanksgiving Service, she recalled that moment in South Africa. "When I was twenty-one, I pledged my life to the service of our people, and I asked God's help to make good that vow. Although that vow was made in my salad days when I was green in judgement, I do not regret nor retract one word of it."

Elizabeth was accompanied on the tour by Princess Margaret, who, as one of the few who were privy to the news of the engagement to Philip, witnessed at first hand the princess's frustration and distress about being so far away from the man she loved for so long. Two months after her return she became publicly engaged to Philip and finally, on 20 November 1947, she married him at Westminster Abbey in a ceremony that Winston Churchill welcomed as "a flash of colour on the hard road we have to travel" – a sombre road thanks to a disastrous winter, the effects of rationing and the beginning of the Cold War.

Romance dominated the summer of 1951, during which Princess Margaret celebrated her twenty-first birthday. William's "Aunt Margot" was one of the dazzling lights of post-war society. She dominated the infamous

"Margaret set" of mostly male aristocratic admirers who escorted her around London's leading nightclubs and restaurants, as well as to the new wave of American musicals. Few realized at the time that her heart lay not with future dukes and marquises, but with her father's equerry, the Battle of Britain fighter pilot, Group Captain Peter Townsend, who was not only married, but – in those class-conscious times – was a mere member of staff and therefore her social inferior. Ironically, forty years later her niece Anne would marry her mother's equerry, Commander Tim Laurence, with relatively few shock waves.

In August 1951 the royal family headed north to Balmoral. One day after a picnic lunch, Townsend was stretched out on the heather having a nap when he woke to find someone covering him with a coat. He opened his eyes to discover Princess Margaret, her face very close to him, staring intently at him. Behind her stood the King, leaning on his stick, studying the two young people with a wry smile on his face. Townsend said, "You know your father is watching us?" The Princess laughed and, still staring at him, she walked towards the King. "Then she took his arm, and walked him away", recalled Townsend, "leaving me to my dreams."

On 21 August, Margaret glided down the stairs of the Victorian castle in a new Christian Dior creation of white organza, which in her later years she still remembered as "a dream of a dress". After dinner she cut her large birthday cake, which had been brought specially by train from London and which was decorated with an icing version of her coat of arms. Afterwards she danced eightsome reels in the ballroom before the party moved outside on to the driveway. Each member of the party was given a torch before they arranged themselves into a long line stretching a hundred yards along the hillside. A flame was passed from torch to torch until the final one was used to ignite a bonfire that estate workers had

Right: Anne in 1971 looking glamorous for a gala dinner. By her late twenties she was noticeably frugal about her clothes, boasting that "a good suit can go on for ever if it's properly made in the first place".

Below: Princess Anne arrives in Kenya, February 1971. It was clear that she had inherited her father's forthright personality and was happier in a shirt and trousers than she was in hats, gloves and pearls.

prepared. Margaret had been the first senior royal baby to be born in Scotland since the future Charles I in 1600. On the night of her birth another bonfire, this time at her ancestral home and birthplace of Glamis castle, had welcomed her safe arrival into the world.

As the summer nights began to draw in, so did the safe world of childhood. A month after Margaret's birthday the King had the whole of his left lung removed after doctors diagnosed a malignant tumour. The following February, after listening to Margaret play some of his favourite tunes on the piano at Sandringham, the King retired to bed in his rooms on the first floor. At some point during the night he died peacefully in his sleep. Between her father's death and her marriage in 1960, Margaret lived at Clarence House with the Queen Mother. Together they helped to look after Charles and Anne during the Queen's frequent absences on overseas tours. After her death in February 2002 Charles would pay a tribute to her as "a wonderfully vibrant woman with such a free spirit."

Above: Prior to 1969, the British public had never heard Prince Charles utter a single word. This was to alter dramatically that summer when the prince gave a creditable radio interview with veteran broadcaster Jack de Manio. The following day huge chunks of the interview were printed verbatim in the press. Bouyed by his success the palace press office organised this BBC TV peak time discussion.

Margaret was one of the chief guests at Charles's own twenty-first birthday party on 14 November 1969 as she had been earlier in the year when the Queen formally invested him as the twenty-first Prince of Wales in a ceremony at Caernarvon Castle in north Wales. On the morning of his birthday, accompanied by his grandmother, Charles arrived at the Chapel Royal of St John in the Tower of London. There, in the chapel where the earliest Princes of Wales had prayed to God, he attended a service of thanksgiving and dedication for his future life.

Unlike his younger brothers who turned Windsor Castle into a disco for the evening, Charles characteristically chose the more sedate option of a concert at Buckingham Palace. The violinist Yehudi Menuhin played a

Right: The investiture of Charles as Prince of Wales at Caernarvon Castle, the highlight of his twenty-first year. "For me", he wrote later, "by far the most moving and meaningful moment came when I put my hands between Mummy's and swore to be her liege man of life and limb and to live and die against all manner of folks – such magnificent, medieval, appropriate words."

Left:Edward spent his twenty-first birthday studying archaeology and anthropology at Cambridge University. "These have been three of the best years of my life", he told the *Cambridge Evening News* that summer. "Everybody says that about school, but I don't think I ever enjoyed school as much as I enjoyed university. There's a wonderful mix of people and I am never likely to mix so informally with such a wide range of people."

Mozart violin concerto, accompanied by the Bath Festival Orchestra, and Maurice Gendron completed the programme with a Haydn cello concerto.

Later a massive firework display illuminated the sky over central London as the four hundred guests crowded the palace gardens to watch. In fact, there were 404 guests, since four Oxford University students gatecrashed the event and enjoyed long chats with Prime Minster Harold Wilson and the birthday boy himself, before being removed as they made their way over to the Queen. She can't have been too concerned about the intrusion, since she was spotted dancing away until 3 a.m. when the party was offered a kedgeree breakfast.

Prince Andrew celebrated his twenty-first birthday at the Royal Naval Air Station at Culdrose in Cornwall where he was training to become a pilot. At the age of twenty-one he was promoted to sub-lieutenant and joined 820 Squadron on HMS *Invincible*. The following spring *Invincible* sailed as part of the task force to liberate the Falkland Islands from Argentine occupation. At twenty-two Andrew became the most recent member of the royal family to see active service.

Four years later Prince Edward reached twenty-one during his final year at Cambridge University, where he made his acting debut playing the judge in Arthur Miller's *The Crucible*. On his birthday the cast and production-team of the show he was currently working on threw a party for him backstage that went on until the small hours. Sadly no photographs exist but he was spotted meandering through the streets of Cambridge in the early hours of the morning, trying to find his way home wearing a bowler hat and clutching his presents.

For Princess Anne, 1971 was one of the most eventful years of her life. In 1970 she had accepted the Presidency of the Save the Children Fund and agreed to travel to Kenya to make a television safari film for the popular BBC children's programme, *Blue Peter*. She landed in Nairobi on 6

Right: Andrew would follow in the footsteps of his brother Charles, his father and his grandfather and enter the Royal Naval College, Dartmouth. He enrolled as a seaman, specializing as a helicopter pilot. At twenty-one he received his helicopter wings from Prince Philip and also won the prize for the best pilot on the course.

February 1971 and trailed by the film crew she made a sentimental journey to Treetops, the lodge in northern Kenya where the Queen had celebrated the nineteenth anniversary of her succession to the throne. As her mother had done before her, Anne sat on the balcony photographing the animals visiting the water hole in the clearing between the trees below her.

During the summer the princess uncharacteristically cancelled a number of engagements at short notice. In early July she collapsed in agony and was rushed to the King Edward VII Hospital for Officers where she underwent an emergency operation for the removal of an ovarian cyst, which had begun to haemorrhage. She was well enough to join her family for the annual cruise of the Western Isles of Scotland in the Royal Yacht Britannia. The itinerary was arranged so that the princess could spend her twenty-first birthday at the Castle of Mey, the Queen Mother's Caithnesshire retreat nine-and-a-half kilometres (six miles) west of John o'Groats. As the yacht docked at Scrabster harbour, the crowd of well-wishers sang "Happy Birthday" as Anne stepped ashore. Her cards and presents had earlier been delivered to her at sea by helicopter .

The following morning Anne flew south to prepare for the European Equestrian Championships. Although she had been left out of the official British team, she was invited to compete as an individual. She accepted the challenge and, against the top riders of nine countries, won the European individual gold medal in faultless style. Newspaper editors, who normally lambasted the princess for famously telling their photographers to "Naff Off!" – or worse – were obliged to bow to their readers' wishes and laud her as Sportswoman of the Year. To crown her success she was also elected Sports Personality of the Year by BBC television viewers. The following year she came from nowhere into third place in a Gallup poll of the world's most admired women, behind her mother and the Israeli Prime Minster Mrs Golda Meir.

The only other British princess to celebrate a twenty-first birthday since 1971 was Diana, Princess of Wales. She spent the day in her apartments at Kensington Palace celebrating with the quietest birthday party of all, having presented the nation with its own fabulous birthday present ten days earlier – Prince William.

Right: The last three generations of the royal family were each launched onto the royal stage by the time they were twenty-one. William is so far resisting this daunting challenge. He will be twenty-three by the time he leaves St Andrews and he is determined to enjoy this period of relative anonymity for as long as he can.

CHAPTER TEN

FUTURE KING

In the natural course of events William will succeed his father to the throne as King William V. At that stage William will be committed to a life of public service and the necessity of being a credit to his country. His future will be mapped out in a series of royal engagements planned up to two years ahead. He will never be able to withdraw from public life in the way that his mother attempted following her separation. If he were to abdicate like Edward VIII he would simply be shifting the burden of kingship on to Harry, and condemning himself to a life of unfulfilling exile with no meaningful role to play, as the Duke of Windsor found to his cost.

In the meantime William will have to try to develop a role for himself that respects his royal heritage but is at the same time true to his mother's beliefs and wishes. This won't be an easy task. As Geordie Greig points out, "There's a lot resting on him, and it remains to be seen whether he will ever be able to have a successful career or whether he will even be able to lead a private life, and of course whatever he does will come in for detailed analysis by the media – one angry spat with the press and they'll retaliate with force." He will graduate from St Andrews in 2005 but his career options will be carefully analyzed long before that.

Both the Queen and Prince Charles began undertaking royal duties at a relatively young age.

Right: Surrounded by the trappings of monarchy, William is learning to balance his needs as an individual with the necessity of taking centre stage as second in line to the throne. Wearing a Golden Jubilee medal William rides in the carriage procession to St Paul's Cathedral for the nation's thanksgiving service, 4 June 2002.

Left: William learned at an early age that he had to repay public adoration with a commitment to duty. On a "walkabout" in Cardiff the nine-year-old prince discovers that meeting the people can be fun.

During the war, Elizabeth was made a Counsellor of State at eighteen, which meant that she had to represent the King when he was away. While he was visiting the troops of the Eighth Army in Italy, Elizabeth had to sign a reprieve for a murderer. Charles was also eighteen when he was given the same role. By the time he reached twenty-one he was a Knight of the Garter, a Privy Councillor and a member of the House of Lords. He had attended three State Openings of Parliament, represented the Queen in Australia and Malta, welcomed the Finnish president at Victoria Station, and had his first death threat – all while studying for his degree finals.

It seems likely that William's launch into the public arena will take far longer. When the prince was seventeen Earl Spencer revealed, "In the

Above: A walkabout in Cardiff in 1991 and William tries to emulate his mother's relaxed informality with the public. Diana would lean forward, whisper conspiratorily to her fans, and giggle at their comments. Behind the naturalness was a carefully honed public relations exercise that won her many admirers.

medium term, William wants to go into the armed forces in some form," adding, "This is a traditional part of the royal upbringing, but he'd actually like to do it of his own volition, so that's great." The earl didn't specify whether it was the army, the navy or the RAF that most interested his nephew, but the indications are that he favours the army. He thoroughly enjoyed the week he spent with the Welsh Guards on a jungle training programme in Belize. At the time "a senior royal courtier" told *The Times*, "It is still very early on, but Prince William is definitely considering going into the army. He loves the outdoors."

Traditionally most royal princes favour the Royal Navy. Prince Charles joined the navy after he graduated from Cambridge and Prince Andrew served as a helicopter pilot in the Falklands War while their father served throughout the Second World War and their grandfather took part in the naval battle of Jutland in 1916.

The last heir to the throne to serve in the army was the Queen's uncle, who, as Prince of Wales, served with the Grenadier Guards during the First World War. He found "It took a long time to become reconciled to the policy of keeping me away from the front line. Manifestly I was being kept, so to speak, on ice, against the day that death should claim my father." Because he was heir to the throne Edward could only "snatch quick glimpses of the devastation of war", and he had to be satisfied with completing a routine desk job, "made work, I soon realized, designed to conceal my non-combatant role under a show of activity." William is probably all too aware that in the event of war, he would be treated in exactly the same way, partly because of the obvious dangers but partly because seizing the Queen's grandson as a prisoner of war would be a coup for any attacking army.

In an interview published to coincide with his arrival at St Andrews, William gave a clue to another area in which he would like to be involved after university. Asked whether his history of art course would help him very much in his career, he replied, "I'm much more interested in doing something with the environment, but I'm not sure what yet." The fact that he loved his time working on a farm during his year off from studying and that he was also in the Agricultural Society at Eton proves that this is an

Left: With the Queen and Prince Philip the oldest generation of the royal family and Prince Charles and the Princess Royal now in their mid-fifties it is down to William to capture the imagination of young people and to make the monarchy relevant to future generations. Here he meets volunteers from the Prince's Trust in Glasgow, September 2001.

area he is likely to focus on at some stage. His grandfather, the Duke of Edinburgh, has been actively involved in conservation and the environment for over half a century and became the first president of the World Wildlife Fund. He has frequently campaigned for the preservation of endangered species and has, just as frequently, been forced into defending his own right to shoot wildlife on the various royal estates – a hobby that William shares. Like all his family William will have to avoid any politically- biased organization, and opt to work for a charity or perhaps carry out research for a voluntary group. Since leaving the navy his uncle, the Duke of York, has worked on a voluntary basis as Special Representative for International Trade and Investment. He is working in support of British Trade International, the government body that supports UK companies trading internationally. It also encourages foreign investment. The Duke's role is to lead UK trade missions abroad and to conduct business-focused tours within Britain.

William's great-grandfather Prince Albert, the future King George VI, was to carve a niche for himself in industrial relations after the First World War. His father's private secretary, Lord Stamfordham, wanted to avoid this political minefield, asking the prince's supporters "Are you going to set the King's son against the King's government?" Albert, as strong-

Below: The way that William dealt with Diana's death when he was only fifteen and his good looks and charm have made the prince popular with older generations. Here he faces a daunting array of Edinburgh millinery during a garden party at the Palace of Holyroodhouse, 3 July 2002.

minded as William is today, was adamant and the courtiers had to give way. In 1919 he became President of the Boy's Welfare Association, which was later widened to become the Industrial Welfare Society. The organization aimed to improve relations between employers and employees by improving working conditions, medical care and facilities such as staff canteens. The society was viewed with suspicion by government officials and trade unionists alike, but the press was supportive. *The Daily Sketch* commented, "Prince Albert looks like being in future the Royalty who will be most in touch with social welfare ... As President of the Industrial Welfare Society, he is taking his duties very seriously and pays visits to fac-

tories and works, but so unostentatiously does he set about things that nothing is heard about his work."

When he took on the job, Albert stipulated that he wanted "no fuss, no publicity, no red carpets." William would probably insist on the same conditions, and he would certainly admire his great grandfather's sheer guts in taking on the establishment of the time which would quite happily have had the whole of Britain's industrial heartland red-carpeted if the prince hadn't stopped it. Albert may have been the hero of the working class to the newspapers but to his sarcastic brothers he was just "the Foreman", the sort of levelling comment that William will have hurled at him from Harry when he adopts a similar role.

In another interview, given when he was eighteen, William made it clear that he will not be undertaking solo royal duties until he finishes his full-time education. "It will be a few years before I do royal engagements although I expect, as in the past, I will sometimes accompany my father." Of course Charles isn't King, and it has been suggested by courtiers that William might learn more by accompanying his grandmother on her tours to give him an idea of the type of visit the Head of State is expected to undertake. In the words of one of her biographers, the Queen "embodies the ideal of un-self-interested duty and service", an ideal that has, over the years, won her a great deal of respect, support and affection. Elizabeth is also, of course, the most widely travelled monarch in British history and has visited an estimated 140 countries in more than fifty years. Both Prince Charles and Princess Anne accompanied their parents on several overseas tours in the late 1960s and early 1970s before embarking on a few joint ones of their own.

It is more than likely that William will follow in his father's footsteps and be taken on a series of organized tours to show him how Britain is run, from 10 Downing Street to the smallest of local government offices. There will also be visits to the law courts, the Stock Exchange, the Bank of England and the regional parliamentary assemblies. While dutifully following royal precedent, William will doubtlessly imbue any role he adopts with the independent Spencer spirit he inherited from his mother. As Earl Spencer, himself no stranger to challenging royal conventions, pointed out,

"He's got to make his own way in life and, if he has got some Spencer blood, he won't be backward in coming forward. He will make his own mark." William made this clear when, at eighteen, he refused the HRH prefix that each of the Queen's children adopted when they came of age. His mother was stripped of her HRH on her divorce, and there were reports at the time that William had said that once he became King one of his first actions would be to restore his mother's title. As it is, for the time being, the second in line to the throne will remain plain "Will Wales" during his time at university.

When it came to deciding the future of the Prince of Wales, the Queen and Prince Philip set up a daunting think tank that met for informal sessions to thrash out a suitable public life for the heir to the throne. The elite of the establishment, including Prime Minister Harold Wilson, Archbishop Ramsey of Canterbury, the Chief of the Defence Staff (who happened to be Philip's uncle Earl Mountbatten), the dean of Windsor and the chairman of the Committee of Vice-Chancellors. According to Jonathan Dimbleby, "By convention – endorsed by both the Duke of Edinburgh and Mountbatten – the Prince of Wales would have to enter one or more of the armed services. The issue was whether he should also go to university, and if so which should have precedence, military service or higher education." Such a rigid streamlining of Charles's future, regardless of his talents or preferences, certainly won't recur with William, who himself chose St Andrew's University and who will decide his future life with the same confidence and determination.

It is possible that William will choose to combine his royal duties with "a second life". Prince Felipe, heir to the Spanish throne, managed to combine royal life with his interest in yachting, his academic studies and a three-year term in the armed forces. The Princess Royal pursued a successful equestrian career while still undertaking a heavy schedule of engagements, going on to represent Britain in three-day eventing at the 1976 Olympic Games. William's godfather, ex-King Constantine of Greece was another Olympic competitor, achieving a gold medal in sailing at the 1960 games, and entering the record books as the first Greek since 1912 to win an Olympic gold medal.

Besides finding a suitable role, the prince has the even more challenging task of finding a suitable partner, especially when he knows that the whole newspaper industry is waiting for him to start dating seriously. When Charles was William's age he explained the difficulty he faced, "because you've got to remember that when you marry, in my position, you're going to marry somebody who perhaps one day is going to become Queen." William typically avoids any lengthy self-justification. When asked whether he had a girlfriend he replied firmly, "I like to keep my private life private," and he's likely to continue to do so. He's mildly amused at stories that he is supposedly desperate to date Britney Spears, or that he had a crush on President Bush's niece Lauren when they had never, in fact, seen each other. The same goes for the "exclusive" that he was a close personal friend of Richard Branson's daughter Holly when they hadn't actually been together since they built sandcastles on Necker when they were eight. Another Sunday newspaper alleged a romance between William and Isabella Anstruther-Gough, which prompted her father to fire off a letter to the Press Complaints Commission pointing out that the young couple had in fact never met. Periodically the tabloids publish a spread of photos of William's "girlfriends" or, more accurately, his non-girlfriends. Labelled "Willie's Fillies" by the media, they usually come from within the same

Left: After graduating in the summer of 2005 it is likely that William will follow his Uncle Andrew's example and opt for a life in the army. Earl Spencer has suggested that he might join the Scots Guards. The prince spent a short time on jungle manoeuvres with the Welsh Guards in Belize in 2000. Andrew and William are driving to St Paul's for the Golden Jubilee service.

Above: Charles has made William aware of royalty's need to be the moral conscience of the nation in the face of catastrophe. The princes sign a book of condolence for the 9/11 victims at the US Consulate in Edinburgh, 21 September 2001.

Overleaf: At one with the people. Jubilee Day, 4 June 2002, and a sea of hands reaches out to touch royalty.

group of striking, blonde, polo-playing young women who live within easy reach of Highgrove.

When he was asked at eighteen how he copes with the attention of girls, William's reply was non-committal. "In my own way. Trying to explain how might be counter-productive!" As for the links with Britney and the show business set, the prince was resolutely downbeat. "There's been a lot of nonsense put about by PR companies. I don't like being exploited in this way but as I get older it's increasingly hard to prevent." He knows from bitter experience how his mother was exploited both before and after her death by friends and lovers and he is naturally suspicious of any new contacts he makes. Speaking just before his arrival at St Andrews he warned that "People who try to take advantage of me and get a piece of me – I spot it quickly and soon go off them." He did, however, give a clue as to how

he chooses his friends – and perhaps girlfriends. "It's not as if I choose my friends on the basis of where they are from or what they are. It's about character and who they are and whether we get on. I just hope I can meet people I get on with. I don't care about their backgrounds."

William's few interviews and official comments show clear insight and firm determination. This strength of mind, combined with the qualities of leadership he developed as a Pop at Eton, and the self-reliance he showed during his time with Raleigh International during his gap year will be a distinct advantage in his future role. He has also demonstrated an interest in issues such as the environment that reflects Charles's wider concerns, and he has inherited both his parents' sensitivity in dealing with all types of people – again a distinct advantage to a future king. As Earl Spencer said about both William and Harry, "They've got quite a lot of their mother in them, in particular their respect for people of whatever background. They're not at all snobbish and I think that's certainly a trait she always had too."

The main disadvantage for William is that unlike the Queen he won't be satisfied in maintaining the status quo. When Elizabeth succeeded to the throne at the age of twenty-five she said, "Everything must continue in the way that it did in my father's reign." And indeed, apart from some streamlining and cost-cutting exercises, the fabric of the monarchy is very similar to how it was in the middle of the twentieth century. It is difficult to imagine William V being surrounded by "Pages of the Backstairs", "Silver Sticks in Waiting", "Lord High Almoners" and the other functionaries that form his grandmother's court. It will be as difficult for William to conform to this rigid structure of monarchy as it was for Edward VIII seventy years ago. "Some Princes bend their characters more easily than others to this rule," he wrote after his abdication in 1936. "It

Above: As three generations of the royal family walk back to Sandringham House after attending a Christmas Day service at St Mary Magdalene church on the estate one eager fan ducks under the ropes to meet her hero. Peter Phillips, walking ahead with Prince Charles, is amused at what has become an annual ritual.

was to be my fate to find it at times irksome because I had been endowed with a questioning, independent mind, and I found it difficult ever to take anything for granted, even my own position."

When Princess Margaret was asked to predict the future of the monarchy, she said simply, "As long as the family can produce nicely brought up young people it will be all right." Thanks to Charles and Diana's example, William was taught that with the vast estates and immense privileges that will always surround him, there comes a serious responsibility to repay something to society in return for this legacy. From his grandmother the Queen and his great grandmother the Queen Mother, who was still carrying out royal engagements at the age of 101, William was also given the finest examples of public duty.

As the old imperial style of monarchy dies away, a new type of monarchy will necessarily establish itself. It is more important than ever that it should reinvent itself by encapsulating the best of the past and making it relevant to the future. With his undoubted intelligence, integrity, sensitivity and strength of mind the one person who is capable of rising to this challenge is William.

Right: Looking to the future. The man born to be king in a moment of reflection. The prince was staying at his grandmother's Palace of Holyroodhouse in Edinburgh. Behind him the craggy granite outcrop of Arthur's Seat dominates the skyline.

CHRONOLOGY

21 June 1982 Prince William is born in the Lindo wing of St Mary's Hospital Paddington, London, at 9.03pm.

4 August 1982 The Prince is christened William Arthur Philip Louis by the Archbishop of Canterbury in the Music Room at Buckingham Palace. The ceremony is held on the Queen Mother's 82nd Birthday.

March 1983 William, aged 9 months, accompanies Charles and Diana on their six-week tour of Australia and New Zealand.

15 September 1984 Diana gives birth to Henry Charles Albert David at St Mary's Hospital. The baby will be known as Harry.

24 September 1985 William, aged 3, joins Mrs Mynor's Nursery School in Notting Hill Gate.

15 January 1987 Aged 4 the prince moves to Wetherby day school.

10 September 1990 William becomes a boarder at Ludgrove Preparatory School in Wokingham, Berkshire.

3 June 1991 William is accidentally hit by a golf club while at Ludgrove and is operated on at Great Ormond Street Children's Hospital, London.

December 1992 It is announced that the Prince and Princess of Wales will separate.

29 June 1994 In an ITV documentary Charles admits to adultery with Camilla Parker Bowles.

September 1995 William starts his first term at Manor House, Eton College.

November 1995 Diana's *Panorama* interview, which William watches in private at Eton.

28 August 1996 The Prince and Princess of Wales are granted a decree absolute.

March 1997 Charles and Diana re-united briefly for William's confirmation into the Church of England, held at St George's Chapel, Windsor.

June 1997 At William's suggestion, Diana auctions many of her dresses in New York and raises over £3 million for charity.

July 1997 William and Harry spend a week with Diana in the South of France, the last time the three of them would holiday together.

31 August 1997 William learns from his father that his mother has been killed in a car crash in Paris.

6 September 1997 William follows his mother's cortege on its processional route to Westminster Abbey for her funeral service.

Later he would join the family for a private internment in the grounds of Althorp House, Diana's childhood home.

Easter 1998 William and Harry join Charles on a tour of Canada and are offered overwhelming support by the press and public.

15 April 1999 William makes his first solo appearance at a public event when he attends the christening of Prince Konstantine Alexios of Greece in London. William is one of the baby's godfathers.

June 1999 The prince passes his driving test. In the spring of 2002 he passed his motorcycle test.

21 June 2000 William celebrates his 18th birthday.

June 2000 William leaves Eton with 12 GCSE's and 3 A-levels.

August 2000 Joins the Welsh Guards for a jungle expedition in Belize, the first of his gap year activities. Afterwards he journeys to Mauritius for a work project.

October 2000 He arrives in Chile for a ten-week stay with a group of volunteers from Raleigh International

January 2001 William spends a month working as a farm hand on a dairy farm near to the Highgrove estate.

7 February 2001 William makes his first public appearance with his father and Camilla Parker Bowles at a reception to mark ten years of the Press Complaints Commission.

March 2001 William spends the next three and a half months touring the African continent on a series of study projects.

23 September 2001 William arrives at St Andrews University on the first day of a four year History of Art course.

30 March 2002 The death of the Queen Mother, William's great grandmother, while William is on a skiing holiday with Charles and Harry at Klosters. William will walk behind her coffin on its way to a lying in state at Westminster Hall, and once again a few days later at her funeral service in Westminster Abbey.

4 June 2002 William attends the Golden Jubilee Thanksgiving Service. On 2 June he attended a special service in honour of the event in Swansea and the following day he attended the Party at the Palace – a pop concert held in the grounds of Buckingham palace.

21 June 2003 William celebrates his 21st birthday.

BIBLIOGRAPHY

Theo Aronson *Princess Margaret: A Biography*

Nigel Blundell *The Boy Who Would be King*

Jennie Bond *Reporting Royalty*

Sarah Bradford *Elizabeth: A Biography of Her Majesty the Queen*

Sarah Bradford *King George VI*

Nicholas Davies *William: King for the 21st Century*

Jonathan Dimbleby *The Prince of Wales: A Biography*

Frances Donaldson *Edward VIII*

Andrew Duncan *The Reality of Monarchy*

Anne Edwards *Diana and the Rise of the House of Spencer*

Valerie Garner *Prince William*

Caroline Graham *Camilla – Her True Story*

Kenneth Harris *The Queen*

Christopher Hibbert *Edward VII – A Portrait*

Brian Hoey *Her Majesty – Fifty Regal Years*

Anthony Holden *Charles at Fifty*

P.D. Jephson *Shadows of a Princess*

Penny Junor *Charles and Diana: Portrait of a Marriage*

Richard Kay *Diana: The Untold Story*

Douglas Keay *Elizabeth II: Portrait of a Monarch*

Angela Levin *Raine and Johnnie: The Spencers and the Scandal of Althorp*

Suzy Menckes *Queen and Country*

Dermot Morrah *The Royal Family in Africa*

Andrew Morton *Diana: Her True Story – In Her Own Words*

Kenneth Rose *King George V*

D & G Strober *The Monarchy: An Oral History of Elizabeth II*

Graham Turner *Elizabeth: The Woman and the Queen*

Christopher Warwick *Princess Margaret*

Ken Wharfe *Diana: Closely Guarded Secrets*

Philip Ziegler *King Edward VIII: The Official Biography*

INDEX

PICTURE ACKNOWLEDGEMENTS

The publisher wishes to thank the organizations listed below for their kind permission to reproduce the photographs in this book. Every effort has been made to acknowledge the pictures, however we apologize if there are any unintentional omissions.

B = bottom; *L* = left; *R* = right; *T* = top.

Alpha Press Images 1, 29, 30, 38, 49, 52, 72-73, 76, 116, 120, 126, 184.

Camera Press 13, 61, 66, 78, 81, 96, 97, 112T, 113T, 122, 123, 131, 145, 173, 177, 188, /BRO/CO 166, 167, /Lionel Cherruault 17T, 19BL, /W. Cheung 171, /Srdja Djukanovic 132, /Richard Gillard 9, 87, 90T, 124, 143, /G. Harvey 168, /I. Jones 138, /Marion Kaplan 164, /Kim Knott 34, /Serge Lemoine 165, /Ian Lloyd 162, /David Long 98-99, /Stewart Mark 48, /R. Open 36B, /Ponopresse 137, /TSPL 39, 154, 155, /The Times 163T, /Vandyk 161.

Corbis 140-141, /Bettmann 15.

Express Syndication 2, 19TR, 37, 54-55, 153.

Getty Images 85R, 160, 163B, 169.

Harlequin Photography 142, 149B.

Ian Lloyd 12, 156-157.

Mirrorpix 21, 23T, 28, 36TL, 43, 51, 62, 68, 82BL, 90B, 100, 102T, 102B, 103, 146, 152, 180, 181.

The Sun/Arthur Edwards 95.

PA Photos 14, 16, 20, 25, 31, 47, 56, 59, 60, 64, 70, 77, 82TR, 83, 105, 110, 111T, 112B, 113B, 114-115, 119, 125, 128, 129, 130, 139, 158, 159, 174, 182-183, 185.

© Photographers International 26-27, 33, 45, 50, 63, 80, 84, 86, 88, 89, 92, 94, 104, 106, 107, 136, 144, 172, /photo by Jane Fincher © A.G. Garrick 22, 42.

Rex 8, 40, 71, 85L, 101, 108, 111B, 118, 135, 148, 149T, 176, 192.

Topham/UPPA 91.

UK Press 10T, 35, 67, 121, 133, 134.